PENTECOSTALS FROM THE INSIDE OUT

PENTECOSTALS FROM THE INSIDE OUT

EDITED BY HAROLD B. SMITH

VICTOR BOOKS®
A DIVISION OF SCRIPTURE PRESS PUBLICATIONS INC.
USA CANADA ENGLAND

All Scripture quotations are from the *King James Version*.

Cover illustration: Tim Jonke

Library of Congress Cataloging-in-Publication Data

Pentecostals from the inside out / edited by Harold Smith.
   p. cm. — (Christianity Today series)
     Includes bibliographical references.
     ISBN 0-89693-544-2
     1. Pentecostals—United States. 2. Pentecostalism—
   United States.
   I. Smith, Harold (Harold B.) II. Series.
   BX8762.A4P46   1990
   289.9′4′0973—dc20   89-28464
                                      CIP

1 2 3 4 5 6 7 8 9 10 Printing/Year 94 93 92 91 90

CONTENTS

PREFACE

This book had its genesis in 1978, when I had the opportunity to meet with Thomas Zimmerman, the then general superintendent of the Assemblies of God, at an annual convention of the National Association of Evangelicals. Breaking every preconceived notion I had about "Holy Rollers" ("weird," uncontrollable, theologically suspect), Dr. Zimmerman spoke the language of faith (with a resonating voice I'll never forget) in terms even this conservative Baptist could freely shout a hearty "Amen" to.

Replacing stereotypes with the truth is the purpose of this volume. And while the truth at times hurts, it is here presented in the hope that both Pentecostals and non-Pentecostals will grow in their understanding of a Spirit-driven movement that has supernaturally advanced God's kingdom to the uttermost parts of the earth.

—*Harold B. Smith,*
general editor

FOREWORD

Long the subject of public ridicule and harassment, Pentecostals by the 1980s had earned the begrudging attention—sometimes even the admiration—of the more staid religious world. No one could have predicted such a scenario in the 1920s. In the early twentieth century, religious observers who were aware that Pentecostals existed labeled them "Holy Rollers," viewed them as faintly berserk, and presumed their bizarre rituals would remain confined to the oak thickets of the outback and slum missions. Who would have believed that these "Holy Rollers" would be the grandparents of sophisticated charismatics and that tongues speaking (upgraded, to be sure, to glossolalia) would reverberate through the ballrooms of Hilton hotels?

Of course, history is filled with ironies; historians explain how it came to pass that the curious became commonplace and the meek inherited the earth. The ironies explored in this book are of no small consequence. The growth of Pentecostal churches and, even more striking, the spread of Pentecostal theology, may be the most important Protestant stories of the twentieth century. Counting religious heads is a tricky business, and some of the exuberant numerical claims of modern charismatics are almost certainly exaggerations.

At best, their estimates of the numbers of Pentecostals/charismatics stretch the meaning of theological categories beyond clear definition; at worst, the numbers become pure boosterism. Nonetheless, any casual observer in the United States will occasionally pass a new multimillion-dollar, space-age sanctuary housing a bulging Pentecostal or charismatic congregation. Outside the United States, from Korea to Chile, the Pentecostal stirring is changing the religious demography of the Christian world.

One of the aims of this book is to identify the Pentecostals of past and present. In part, that is a theological story. In some ways, early Pentecostals were no more than the most fervent wing of nineteenth-century American evangelicalism. They shared with other evangelicals an intense eschatology, seeing themselves as heralds of the end times. Some evangelicals agreed with Pentecostal beliefs in divine healing and the miraculous intervention of God in human affairs. But those conventional beliefs combined in the Pentecostal mind with a more original theology of the Holy Spirit, a "full gospel" that emphasized the gifts of the Spirit. It was this craving for the baptism of the Holy Spirit that set Pentecostals apart from other evangelicals. The first Pentecostals defined themselves, and alienated themselves, by arguing that speaking in tongues was the "initial evidence" of the baptism of the Holy Spirit.

Early Pentecostal beliefs were nurtured in a distinctive sociological subculture. While Pentecostals might regard themselves as evangelical Christians who had received a higher divine empowering, they were ostracized from early twentieth-century evangelicalism by their beliefs. But Pentecostals were also alienated economically and culturally. Their little churches began and grew among the nation's most depressed and deprived citizens. Pentecostalism did not cause social alienation; it attracted those who were social outcasts. Before World War II, Pentecostalism was pretty well quarantined in enclaves of deprivation. Its churches offered havens of security from the outside world and a degree of self-respect and professional opportunity for the talented poor who had no access to society's established institutions. Every Pentecostal youngster grew to maturity knowing that he was not of the world. He was well aware that his neighbors chuckled under their breath at the spiritual ecstacy that rocked the cinder-block churches on the back streets.

The Pentecostal movement has undergone sweeping changes since World War II. The generation of young Pentecostals who worked in the factories and shipyards of the early 1940s unleashed a pan-Pentecostal revival in the postwar years. They laid aside many of the quirky doctrinal issues that had divided their parents into scores of bickering sects and began to reemphasize their common heritage in the Holy Spirit. When the National Association of Evangelicals was formed in 1943, Pentecostals were for the first time received into a major evangelical association. In 1948, eight of the larger Pentecostal churches formed the Pentecostal Fellowship of North America. By the 1950s, Pentecostals were also supporting important new pan-Pentecostal parachurch organizations, including the healing ministry of Oral Roberts and the Full Gospel Business Men's Fellowship International, an association of laymen. By the middle of the 1950s, the Pentecostal movement had spawned a worldwide revival of interest in faith healing and the baptism of the Holy Spirit.

The modern charismatic movement began with the stunning revelation that the Pentecostal experience had been accepted by mainstream Christians. The first celebrity of the movement was Dennis Bennett, an Episcopal priest who in 1960 attracted national media attention by announcing that he had spoken in tongues. In 1966, a group of students at Notre Dame University triggered the charismatic renewal in the Roman Catholic church. In the three decades since those pioneering experiences, millions of mainstream Protestants and Roman Catholics have been influenced, directly or indirectly, by the Pentecostal emphasis on the Holy Spirit.

The success of Pentecostals and charismatics since World War II complicates the task of understanding the movement. For a time in the 1960s and 1970s the charismatic revival overflowed traditional religious barriers. The joyous embracing of the Holy Spirit ignited extraordinary ecumenical experiences, gatherings small and large that pushed into the background old theological and denominational distinctions. Catholics and Protestants, rich and poor, black and white mingled freely, sharing the gifts of the Holy Spirit. But as the white heat of the revival cooled in the 1980s, charismatics and Pentecostals began to look again at the vast theological, liturgical, and cultural differences that lay beneath their charismatic experiences. If the Holy Spirit united, history and culture still divided. In the 1980s, many who spoke in tongues did not speak to one another.

In short, the growth of the Pentecostal denominations, the spread of the Pentecostal theology of the gifts of the Holy Spirit, and the embrace of the joyous form of Pentecostal worship by mainstream Protestants and Catholics raised countless new problems of definition. What are the similarities and disparities of the many different groups that have embraced the baptism of the Holy Spirit? In what sense is there still a "movement"? In what ways can one identify traditional Roman Catholics, who have embraced a theology of spiritual gifts, with Pentecostals, who retain a prophetic disdain for the Roman Catholic church? In sum, is there any such thing as a Pentecostal/charismatic religious family? If so, what are its dimensions and its core beliefs? The articles in this book explore such questions, though they do not pretend to settle them.

Pentecostalism impinges powerfully on contemporary American and world religion, demanding attention to these questions of definition and history. Nowhere has Pentecostalism left a deeper mark on history than in the rebirth of interest in a theology of the Holy Spirit, an interest that has united Christians from vastly different backgrounds. At the same time, the substantial disagreements between charismatic and Pentecostal theologies of the Holy Spirit have created major barriers between those communities.

Early Pentecostal theology was formulated by unsophisticated preachers who had a limited knowledge of historical Christian thought. Their theology of the Holy Spirit, with its emphasis on the "initial evidence" of speaking in tongues, has been critiqued and discarded by a generation of charismatics, and by many second- and third-generation Pentecostals. And yet, to many modern Pentecostals, "the baptism" remains the hallmark of what it means to be Pentecostal. Even more controversial have been the more eccentric supernatural beliefs that are inherent in the history (and perhaps in the theology) of the Pentecostal subculture—a heritage of demonic and angelic visitations, of supernatural prophets and gifted seers, of healing lines and prosperity messages. Often discarded as "cultural baggage" by sophisticated charismatics, such supernaturalism remains at the heart of many Pentecostal churches and is central to the growth of the movement in the Third World.

At the same time, the charismatic movement and the Catholic Renewal movement have turned the attention of serious scholars and churchmen to the Holy Spirit; they have spent two decades grounding the Pentecostal experience in biblical scholarship and historical theology. Shocked by Pentecostal faith teachers such as Kenneth Hagin and Kenneth Copeland, who are regarded as unsavory extremists, and embarrassed by the grandiose personal experiences of Oral Roberts, these moderate charismatics have searched for guidelines to try the Spirit without quenching the Spirit. As a result, the Pentecostal/charismatic movement of the 1980s is so theologically and culturally diverse (even in the crucial area of understanding the working of the Holy Spirit) that it remains a movement only in terms of historical connections and common roots. Of course, such a statement probably describes every religious family that has reached the stately age of one hundred.

The divisions in the Pentecostal/charismatic movement are institutional as well as theological. From its earliest days, Pentecostalism flourished in a state of spiritual anarchy created by the subjective leading of the Holy Spirit. Divided into scores of little sects, each loyal to the insights of its charismatic leaders, early Pentecostals were rarely able to focus on their common beliefs. Modern Pentecostalism has done little better. While the historic Pentecostal denominations, such as the Assemblies of God, have become more irenic and ecumenical (and, some would argue, less Pentecostal), Pentecostalism in the 1980s continues to shelter a staggering variety of independent churches and fellowships, some of them among the largest megachurches in the nation. More often than not, these rambunctious Pentecostal churches are unfriendly competitors rather than fellow travelers.

Even more insular in the 1980s were the charismatic Christians within the historic churches. Many Protestant denominations reacted negatively to the early charismatic movement, but by the mid-1970s most had come to welcome (or tolerate) charismatics. Partly, there was a growing sense that the charismatics did not threaten the denomination, and, partly, churches reacted in institutional self-defense to stem the flow of members to Pentecostal and independent charismatic churches. By the 1980s, most Protestant churches, and the Roman Catholic church, had well-defined charismatic communities. In most cases, those communities were loyal to their denominational heritage and showed little inclination to abandon church and tradition. It was entirely possible in the 1980s to be a Methodist charismatic, or a part of the Catholic Renewal movement, without ever having heard a Pentecostal preacher or visited a Pentecostal church.

Like all revivals, the Pentecostal/charismatic revival in America created scores of parachurch institutions that momentarily gave the movement cohesion. Few Pentecostals in the 1950s or charismatics in the 1960s were untouched by one of the huge revival ministries headed by evangelists such as Oral Roberts and T. L. Osborne, or by the Full Gospel Business Men's Fellowship International, or by publications such as the *Voice of Healing* and *Abundant Life*. And in the 1970s and 1980s the far-flung movement was given shape by publications such as *Charisma* and by the burgeoning television empires of Roberts, Jimmy Swaggart, Jim Bakker, Pat Robertson, and scores of others.

All of these independent enterprises strove to attract supporters from throughout the Pentecostal/charismatic world; in doing so, they gave unity to the expanding and widening movement. Some were more successful than others. At the beginning of the 1980s, Oral Roberts University came close to being a liberal-arts school for the entire movement, but it became less and less clear as the decade wore on whether the school would be able to maintain such high ground in the dividing movement, or whether the Roberts family would allow it to do so. The FGBMFI continued to have influence across the movement in the 1980s, but internal dissension and competition from other parachurch organizations diminished the fellowship's visibility. Pat Robertson's "The 700 Club" reached a diverse Pentecostal/charismatic clientele in the 1980s, but Robertson's political agenda detracted from his image as a leader of the charismatic movement. In short, the parachurch organizations increasingly came to target certain sections of the Pentecostal/charismatic family to build core constituencies. The jumble of Pentecostals and charismatics in the 1980s no longer read the same magazines, listened to the same preachers, or watched the same television channels.

What, then, has been the impact of the Pentecostal movement in the twentieth century? The articles in this book make it clear that the movement has altered the modern religious world in a variety of ways. In mainstream Protestant denominations and the Roman Catholic church the Pentecostal revival has renewed theological interest in the Holy Spirit and added cells of rejuvenated Christians in thousands of traditional congregations. The historic Pentecostal denominations, led by the Assemblies of God, have been flooded with new members seeking a deeper religious experience, and hundreds of independent Pentecostal and charismatic congregations have been founded by Spirit-filled ministers. The most talented and enterprising Pentecostal and charismatic evangelists have embraced television, following the trailblazing paths of Rex Humbard and Oral Roberts. They have attracted hundreds of thousands of supporters and built empires worth hundreds of millions of dollars. Whatever the future of Pentecostal theology, the great twentieth-century revival has created denominations and independent institutions that will influence the future of Christianity. Those churches and institutions now have distinctive and diverging histories, but the Assemblies of God will play a role in the next century, as will Oral Roberts University and the Christian Broadcasting Network.

Finally, the impact of the American Pentecostal revival outside the United States is just beginning to become apparent. Pentecostal denominations have grown in the Third World, but the charismatic explosion in developing countries is not simply a product of Pentecostal mission work. Nor are most Third World Pentecostals identified with American denominations; they are members of independent and indigenous churches. Nonetheless, these movements bear the theological and cultural marks of the flamboyant moving of the Spirit in America, and their histories will ultimately be written as innovative extensions of the American experience.

In short, the Pentecostal/charismatic movement in the United States that began as a gushing stream in the early twentieth century has now widened into a broad and imposing river. For all of its swiftness at the end of the 1980s, the flow has slowed somewhat, and one can hardly see from one bank of the river to the other. But this expansive river continues to overflow its banks. Both inside and outside the United States, the current still spills into narrow rivulets, surging and roaring into receptive crevices in virgin lands.

More and more those new streams are fed by their own wells of the Spirit, but most owe their beginnings to the great river of American Pentecostalism.

—David Edwin Harrell, Jr.
Birmingham, Alabama

AMERICA'S PENTECOSTALS: WHO THEY ARE

Chapter 1

"WILD THEORIES AND MAD EXCITEMENT"

Grant Wacker

O n a foggy evening in April 1906, a handful of black saints gathered in a small house in Los Angeles to seek the baptism in the Holy Ghost. Before the evening was over, they were singing and shouting in strange languages. Several days later the group moved to an abandoned warehouse on Azusa Street in a run-down section of the city. Soon they were discovered by a *Los Angeles Times* reporter. The "night is made hideous . . . by the howlings of the worshippers," he wrote. "The devotees of the weird doctrine practice the most fanatical rites, preach the wildest theories and work themselves into a state of mad excitement."

From these inauspicious beginnings, Pentecostalism has mushroomed into the largest Christian movement in the twentieth century. No one knows how big it really is, but the statistics are staggering. David B. Barrett's *World Christian Encyclopedia* lists more than 300 million adherents worldwide. The three largest Protestant congregations in the world are Pentecostal, including Paul Cho's Full Gospel Central Church in Seoul, Korea, which boasts 500 thousand weekly attenders, 370 thousand members, and 50 thousand neighborhood prayer cells. A 1979 Gallup poll revealed that in the United States alone, 19 percent—or 29 million—adult Americans considered themselves "Pentecostal or charismatic Christians." Of these, five million claimed to have experienced the hallmark of the Pentecostal tradition, speaking in "unknown tongues," technically called *glossolalia*.

In this country, one-third of those who identify themselves as Pentecostal belong to one of the 300 or so historically Pentecostal denominations. Most are quite small, yet the two largest, the Church of God in Christ and the Assemblies of God, claim 3.7 and 2.1 million constituents respectively. The validity of the former figure has been disputed. But there can be little doubt that the Assemblies of God, which numbers an additional 16 million followers in overseas affiliates, ranks among the strongest and proportionately wealthiest denominations in the world.

Respectability seems to have grown with the numbers. David Edwin Harrell recently ranked Oral Roberts with Billy Graham as one of the two most influential religious leaders of the twentieth century. And when Pentecostal spokesman David J. du Plessis died in February 1987, he clearly commanded a degree of esteem among world ecumenical leaders that would have been inconceivable a generation earlier.

Just what is Pentecostalism?
Immensity breeds confusion. Contemporary Pentecostalism is so vast and sprawling it is sometimes difficult for outsiders to know exactly what the creature is. Like the beasts in Noah's ark, Pentecostals come in a bewildering variety. Protestant, Catholic, Reformed, Wesleyan, Trinitarian, Unitarian, mainline, sectarian, white, black, Hispanic, nouveau riche, working class—the list of adjectives that describe one subgroup or another could be extended almost indefinitely. Perhaps more than any other segment of Christendom, the boundaries of the movement seem hopelessly tangled in a maze of

crisscrossing beliefs and practices.

There is, however, at least one conviction that all Pentecostals share, virtually by definition. Conversion to Christ must be followed by another life-transforming event known as baptism, or filling, by the Holy Spirit. Exactly how this experience is manifested in the life of the believer is a subject of endless dispute. In general, the older or "classical" Pentecostal groups insist that all Christians will speak in unknown tongues at the moment of baptism. They call this the sign or evidence of baptism, and believe that it always takes place when a person has been filled by the Spirit.

Classical Pentecostals also maintain that a Spirit-filled person normally will manifest one or more of the nine gifts of the Spirit described in 1 Corinthians 12 and 14. These include the gift of tongues, which may be used more or less at will for private or public prayer (as distinguished from the sign of tongues, which invariably accompanies the baptism in the Holy Spirit).

There are exceptions and differing emphases among Pentecostals even on these matters. Black Pentecostals are distinguished more by their music than by speaking in tongues,* and Roman Catholic and some Protestant bodies in South America and Europe argue that tongues is one of many possible manifestations of the Spirit's presence. Even so, Pentecostals in all denominations and in all parts of the world agree that baptism in the Holy Spirit ought to be the bare beginning of a triumphant Christian life. And in that life the supernatural power of the Spirit functions not as a deluxe edition of Christianity, reserved only for a few, but as part of God's plan for all of his people.

It should be noted that this description of Pentecostalism focuses upon the beliefs that distinguish these from other evangelical Christians. The point here is that the movement is better described by its beliefs than by its practices. Contrary to stereotype, Pentecostals are deadly serious about correct doctrine. They habitually define them-

---

*Vinson Synan, author of *Holiness-Pentecostal Movement in the United States*, notes that black contributions in the area of music are often overlooked. Perhaps the most widely sung hymns coming out of black Pentecostalism are those of Thoro Harris, who wrote, "Jesus Loves the Little Children," "All That Thrills My Soul Is Jesus," and "He's Coming Soon." From the holiness tradition came such hymns as "Deeper, Deeper," "I'm Happy With Jesus Alone," "I Would Not Be Denied," and "Come Unto Me," all by C. P. Jones. And G. T. Haywood, the oneness leader, wrote hymns that included "I See a Crimson Stream of Blood" and "Jesus the Son of God."

selves in doctrinal terms, and some of the deepest wounds they have inflicted upon themselves have come from brawls over technicalities of belief.

Nonetheless, a purely doctrinal definition is too thin. For many years Pentecostalism was a total style of life, a way of seeing and feeling and experiencing reality. The driving force was, as Perry Miller said of the Puritans, not in its beliefs but behind them, in the spirituality that sparked the movement and the certitude that sustained it.

In the beginning: Colliding notions

Historians commonly trace the movement's origins to the social and cultural crises of the late nineteenth century. As the stable structures of small-town society gave way, and as mainline Protestantism grew soft and fat, the argument runs, Pentecostalism emerged as a plain-folks religion where simple virtues were practiced and the old-fashioned gospel was preached. There is merit in this view, for it is undeniable that the movement initially flourished in regions suffering severe disruption of traditional ways. Nonetheless, the forces that gave birth to Pentecostalism were broader and deeper than the social and cultural shock waves of the 1890s.

To a great extent, the movement grew from the confluence of five distinct theological currents that had been churning within the holiness and higher-life movements in Britain and North America for several decades. To begin with, Pentecostalism drew upon the Wesleyan idea of sanctification as it was hammered out in the Methodist holiness tradition. John Wesley had taught that conversion, or the New Birth, was the beginning of a lifelong process of moral perfection. Even so, corrupt desires persisted. This "inbred sin" had to be eradicated in a definable second moment of grace, or "second blessing," in which the stranglehold of sin was decisively broken. "Be of sin the double cure," it was phrased in a hymn long cherished by Methodists; "Save from wrath and make me pure."

Pentecostalism also drew upon a closely related tradition that was rooted in the teachings of evangelist Charles G. Finney and other Presbyterian and Congregationalist writers. These higher-life advocates, as they were known, similarly emphasized the importance of a life-transforming experience after conversion. However, they understood it not as a second moment of grace that eradicated sinful desires, but as an enduement of power that equipped the believer for witness and service. By the end of the nineteenth century, this second crisis experience in the spiritual life of the believer generally came to be called, in both the holiness and higher-life traditions, the baptism in (or of) the Holy Spirit.

The third and fourth streams that led to Pentecostalism were dispensational premillennialism and a new theology of divine healing. The former entailed the idea of an imminent secret rapture of the saints, immediately followed by seven years of great tribulation, the second coming of the Lord, and the millennium. It stemmed from the teachings of the Plymouth Brethren, and it was articulated by well-known preachers such as Reuben Archer Torrey.

The new theology of divine healing departed from historic Christian doctrine (which had enjoined elders to anoint and pray for the sick) by insisting that Christ's atonement provided healing for the body just as it provided healing for the soul. This idea was popularized especially by A. B. Simpson, founder of the Christian and Missionary Alliance, and by independent divine healers such as John Alexander Dowie and Maria B. Woodworth-Etter.

The fifth, and probably the most important, current that influenced Pentecostalism was a great longing for restoration of the power and miracles of the New Testament church. Many expected that the "former rain," the signs and wonders described in Acts, soon would be complemented by the "latter rain," a final outpouring of the Holy Spirit's power at the close of history. The origins of this influence are difficult to pin down, but nineteenth-century evangelical Protestantism was peppered with the same restorationist ideas that strongly affected other indigenous groups such as Churches of Christ and the Latter-day Saints.

The movement organizes

As the century drew to a close, these various notions collided, broke apart, and reassembled in unpredictable ways. But by 1900, many who sought a deeper Christian experience in one tradition or another became persuaded that the growing hunger for the baptism in the Holy Spirit was a token of the Lord's imminent return. At the same time, the astonishing growth of divine-healing experiences in the 1880s and 1890s stirred expectations that other New Testament miracles soon would be restored.

And then there was the revival setting. In the "fire-baptized holiness" meetings of the late 1890s, one leader remembered, the "people screamed until you could hear them for three miles on a clear night, and until the blood vessels stood out like whip cords." A newspaper reporter who visited Maria Woodworth-Etter's meetings wrote that one could not "imagine the confusion." Another reporter judged that her services sounded like the "female ward of an insane asylum." In contexts of this sort, it was only a matter of time until some believers began to look for proof—palpable proof—that they truly had been baptized in the Holy Spirit and thus were ready for the Lord's return.

No one knows when speaking in tongues first erupted. There is considerable disagreement among scholars about whether it was or was not a regular feature within holiness and higher-life circles (although there is no question that it was widely practiced among the Latter-day Saints). In any event, the distinctive claim of modern Pentecostalism—that the baptism in the Holy Spirit always is signified by unknown tongues—can be traced to a revival in Topeka, Kansas, in 1901. In that stirring, an itinerant healer named Charles Fox Parham taught that in Acts, tongues accompanied all instances of baptism in the Holy Spirit, either explicitly or implicitly, and therefore that pattern should be normative for Christians today. In 1905, Parham migrated to Houston, where he influenced William J. Seymour, a black evangelist associated with a holiness and restorationist band called the Evening Light Saints. Seymour, in turn, carried the message to Los Angeles, where his preaching sparked the now legendary Azusa Street revival the following spring.

Between 1906 and 1911, several small but thriving Wesleyan sects in the Southeast were drawn into Pentecostalism through the influence of persons who had visited the Azusa Street Mission. These included, among others, the predominantly black Church of God in Christ, the Church of God (Cleveland, Tenn.), and the Pentecostal Holiness Church. Over the years, these Wesleyan-based groups have remained strongest in the Southeast.

After a slow start, the Pentecostal message caught fire among Reformed (that is, non-Wesleyan) Christians in the central states. In

1914 several thousand independent believers in the lower Midwest joined with converts in the Christian and Missionary Alliance in the upper Midwest to form the Assemblies of God. Two years later, a schism in that denomination over the nature of the Trinity prompted the formation of several Unitarian or "Oneness" groups. The largest of the latter are the United Pentecostal Church and the largely black Pentecostal Assemblies of the World. Aimee Semple McPherson also launched her ministry in the Assemblies of God, but she soon broke away to establish her own following in Los Angeles, incorporated in 1927 as the Church of the Foursquare Gospel.

The charismatic movement

One of the most remarkable and least predictable religious developments in the past generation has been the penetration of speaking in tongues and other Pentecostal distinctives into some of the mainstream Protestant denominations and the Roman Catholic church. While classical Pentecostals remain clustered in the working and lower middle classes, there are no appreciable social or demographic differences between these newer "charismatic Christians," as they usually call themselves, and the general population.

The origin of the charismatic movement is commonly traced to the ministry of Dennis Bennett, rector of Saint Mark's Episcopal Church in Van Nuys, California, who received the Pentecostal experience in 1959. From this nucleus it rapidly spread to other denominations, including the Roman Catholic church. Paradoxically, perhaps, the movement showed greatest success among "high church" bodies such as Catholic, Episcopalian, and Lutheran, and least among "low church" bodies such as Southern Baptist and Nazarene.

By the mid-1960s, charismatic prayer cells were dotting the nation's campuses as well. Here, too, the movement seems to have grown most luxuriantly in the least likely places, first taking root in the prestigious colleges and seminaries of the Northeast, and in Catholic universities such as Duquesne, Fordham, and Notre Dame.

Whether the charismatic movement stemmed from the soil of classical Pentecostalism or whether it represented an indigenous development within the mainstream Protestant and Roman Catholic traditions is debatable. What seems beyond dispute, however, is that groups such as the Full Gospel Business Men's Fellowship provided a bridge linking the older and newer forms of Pentecostal piety. Founded in Los Angeles in 1951 by a wealthy dairyman named Demos Shakarian, the fellowship's nondenominational monthly meetings gave laypersons and ministers an opportunity for independent prayer and testimony. This arrangement proved attractive to believers who had received the Pentecostal experience yet wished to remain loyal to their own churches. By 1980, the fellowship posted 2,300 chapters in twenty-seven countries. Mainline Protestants and Roman Catholics constituted the majority of its membership.

The vision blurred

Today the Pentecostal movement is more diverse than ever. Deep theological and cultural differences separate the newer charismatic from the older classical groups. And within the latter, the fractures are just as deep. The rift between Wesleyan bodies (such as the Pentecostal Holiness Church) and the Reformed bodies (such as the Assemblies of God) began to heal with the formation of the Pentecostal Fellowship of North America in 1948 and the scholarly Society for Pentecostal Studies in 1970. But other rifts, such as that between the Trinitarian majority and the large Oneness minority, persist. Each warily eyes the other with the suspicion that it is sub-Christian at best.

Yet the most intractable breaches are sociological and cultural rather than theological. Black and white Pentecostals are still mostly segregated. Fiercely independent outposts in skid-row missions and Appalachian hollows contrast with opulent suburban churches and, of course, even more opulent parachurch ministries. Since the 1950s, countless rank-and-file believers have strayed into other pastures, sharing their loyalties—and wallets—with independent "prosperity" evangelists such as Kenneth Copeland and Richard Roberts, who preach faith as an avenue to financial success.

Increasing internal diversity and spiraling numbers tell only part of the story, however. If there is a single message that emerges from an overview of the history of Pentecostalism, it is that the movement has come perilously close to shifting its focus from the "full gospel" of the early days to a preoccupation with conservative social and political causes and adulation of such politically conservative celebrities as Pat Boone and former Secretary of the Interior James Watt. Still more striking is the development of an explicit commitment to the pursuit of health, wealth, and worldly success under the aegis of prosperity evangelism.

Not surprisingly, denominational officials are acknowledging and lamenting that change: for example, in an interview with CHRIS-TIANITY TODAY, G. Raymond Carlson, general superintendent of the Assemblies of God, condemned the "name it–claim it" teaching as being "steeped in a very humanistic, me-first, materialistic kind of orientation rather than an orientation to Christ and him crucified." And Ray Hughes, former head of the Church of God (Cleveland, Tenn.), agreed. Said Hughes, "The people are so engaged in making money, subconsciously mammon has become their god until this has clouded, in many places, the real fervor, fire, and New Testament zeal that comes with Pentecostal experience." Hughes believes Pentecostalism has a special calling to avoid materialism: "Most of us classic Pentecostals came from the blue-collar, working-class group. And the thing that made Pentecostalism grow was that they took the gospel to the poor. We must never forget our roots, regardless of how the gospel has lifted us materially." (See Appendix 1, "Growing Up Pentecostal," pp. 141-144.)

The historical record leaves little doubt that Pentecostals have not tried very hard to resist the temptations of the good life. The well-known revelations about the lifestyle of Jim and Tammy Bakker illustrate the point. Describing this latter aspect of contemporary Pentecostalism as a "veritable spiritual Amway movement," historian Harrell notes that it offers not healing for the sick, but security for the well; not consolation to the poor, but confirmation to the successful.

All in all, then, Pentecostalism has paid a steep price for moving uptown. Its uncritical identification with the values of middle America represents a major loss of prophetic vision. In 1976, church historian Martin E. Marty perceptively noted that in times past Pentecostalism "was 'true' because it was small and pure, but now it is 'true' because so many are drawn to it."

The vision recovered?
Having said all this, it is important to add that the story of American Pentecostalism is not adequately grasped if we think of it only in

sociological terms as a sect quietly drifting back into the mainstream of respectable Protestantism. For one thing, there are numerous exceptions. Every day countless Pentecostals put their lives squarely behind their ideals, giving a tithe or more of their time and money to the work of the church. In 1986, for example, the Assemblies of God alone devoted $135 million, or 74 percent of its total expenditures, to world ministries, outstripping the per capita giving of any mainline group.

Moreover, while accommodation to the values of middle America may be the central trend of American Pentecostalism since World War II, it would be unfair to say that was true of the first and second generations. The work of the pioneers is best understood not as compensation for poverty or low social status, but as a burst of radical perfectionism. Their faith was not an instrument for escaping life's difficulties but a means for transcending them. Like all truly perfectionist movements in Christian history, early Pentecostalism tried to cope with sin and suffering by forging a new vision of what the gospel was all about. It was a faith to live by, not because it told the truth about this thing or that, but because for the true believer it proved to be, as G. K. Chesterton said of Christianity itself, a "truth-telling thing."

In crucial respects, the Pentecostal movement is less mature today than it was in the early years. Modern Pentecostals do not need to romanticize their past in order to learn from it. The first generation resisted the blandishments of secular society in order to preach a gospel that challenged the culture in more than superficial ways. Modern Pentecostals might recover that vision. They might discover, as church historian George Marsden has put it, that grace is not cheap and that forgiveness is more than good manners. They might discover that in the beginning, the movement survived not in spite of the fact that it was out of step with the times, but precisely because it was.

Chapter 2

THE MOVERS AND SHAKERS

William W. Menzies

I t is little wonder that Pentecostals freely acknowledge the Holy Spirit as the prime mover in their enormous movement—after all, look at the host of individuals he used in making the renewal come alive. Some of these people, as we have already seen, were unlikely candidates, indeed.*

The Azusa Street "transformers"
The most likely candidate for nomination as father of the modern Pentecostal movement is **Charles Fox Parham** (1873–1929). In 1898, he and his young bride established the Beth-el Healing Home in

---

*One window on history is to study the lives of those individuals who had a shaping influence on the movement under investigation. This poses special problems for students of Pentecostal history, since there does not appear to be any single "father" of the movement. There are

Topeka, Kansas. Here he began to publish a bimonthly holiness paper entitled *Apostolic Faith*, the name that became identified with the subsequent Pentecostal movement.

Following a summer tour of holiness-oriented groups in the eastern United States, during which time he became convinced that tongues was the biblical "sign" of Spirit baptism, Parham returned to Topeka. He opened an informal Bible school, and during the fall months of 1900 urged students to search the Scriptures for the biblical teaching regarding this experience. On January 1, 1901, one of his students, Agnes Ozman, received the blessing. Within days Parham, along with many of the students, reported the same experience.

By 1906, Parham, with more than eight thousand followers, was clearly the principal leader of the Pentecostal movement in the Midwest. This was the zenith of his influence. His desire to organize the many Pentecostal missions into a national federation was not to be, however. By the time he arrived in Los Angeles at the Azusa Street Mission, pastored by William J. Seymour, it was too late. Seymour and his colleagues spurned the leadership Parham offered. A morals charge, brought against him in Texas the next year, was never proved and eventually dropped. It nonetheless destroyed his influence. He retired to Baxter Springs, Kansas, where he led a relatively small cluster of devoted disciples. There he died in virtual obscurity.

William Joseph Seymour (1870–1922), the leader of the Azusa Street Mission in Los Angeles, deserves special recognition, for it was from this launching pad that the Pentecostal revival became a worldwide phenomenon. Seymour, a black, was born in Centerville, Louisiana, to former slaves. Though a Baptist early on, he joined a black Methodist church in 1895. Five years later, Seymour fell under the influence of holiness advocates in Cincinnati. There he adopted the teaching of entire sanctification and joined the "Evening Light Saints" (the Church of God, Anderson, Ind.).

In 1903, Seymour moved to Houston, Texas, in an attempt to

---

complex threads that one discovers in the tapestry of the revival, each claiming a cluster of significant personalities important in the shaping of that particular strand. I have, therefore, selected several personalities that may be seen as representative of types or patterns. Other scholars could easily choose a somewhat different list.

locate members of his family. He attended, and later pastored, a holiness church there. When Parham opened his Houston Bible school in December of that year, Seymour enrolled. Yet to satisfy racial segregation requirements, he was only permitted to attend classes by sitting in the hall outside the classroom door. Seymour accepted Parham's teaching that the sign of baptism in the Spirit is tongues, but he did not actually receive the experience until his arrival some weeks later in Los Angeles.

While still pastoring in Houston, Seymour was invited to candidate for the pastorate of a holiness mission in Los Angeles. He was, however, literally locked out of the church because his tongues teaching was a sore offense to the Southern California Holiness Association, of which the mission was a part.

Seymour found comfort in the home of Richard Asberry on Bonnie Brae Street (although Asberry himself did not accept Seymour's Pentecostal teaching). There, a revival broke out, with Seymour and others receiving the Pentecostal blessing. Scores of people came to hear the preaching and testimonies ringing out from the front porch of the house. So many came, in fact, that it soon became necessary to find more suitable quarters. A badly neglected stable and warehouse was obtained at 312 Azusa Street.

Seymour led the first service at the Azusa Street Mission in April 1906. The meetings, marked by noise, some fanaticism, and uncertain teaching, led Seymour to call for help. He invited Parham to come in the fall of 1906, with a view to bringing stability to the revival. However, Parham—deeply offended by the confusion, the noise, and what seemed to him to be spiritualist influences—denounced the proceedings. Perhaps it was his pompous manner, but Parham's attempts at correction were repudiated by the elders, leading to a permanent break between him and Seymour.

The meetings continued for another three years—night and day—attracting worldwide attention. Seymour incorporated the revival as the Pacific Apostolic Faith Movement in 1906. Uneducated as he was, Seymour also began publication that year of a periodical entitled, like Parham's, *Apostolic Faith*. At its zenith, the publication had a worldwide circulation of 50 thousand.

Virtually every ethnic group found in Los Angeles at that time worshiped together in harmony—a phenomenon in the "Jim Crow" era. Remarkable, too, were the testimonies of God's power present in these meetings. Attracted to this humble meeting place, to services led by an ill-educated black, the son of ex-slaves, came missionaries and Christian leaders from many places.

In 1908, Florence Crawford and her colleagues, who worked with Seymour in Los Angeles, took offense at his marriage. They believed the Rapture was coming soon and looked upon his marriage as inappropriate. Crawford took the mailing list for Seymour's periodical to Portland, Oregon, causing a division that proved a severe blow to Seymour's leadership.

Two years later, Seymour's influence suffered yet another setback. William Durham of Chicago came to Los Angeles, propagating the "finished work" teaching, which undermined the view that sanctification is a second work of grace. Durham drew a large part of Seymour's following with him. This effectively ended the significant phase of Seymour's influence. He continued to pastor the Azusa Street Mission until his death in 1922. But for at least the last seven of those years, the church lost its multiracial character and became a strictly black congregation. Pentecostalism had acculturated to segregation.

The holiness pioneers

Between 1907 and 1909, a cluster of Wesleyan-oriented (holiness) bodies, spinoffs of the Methodist church and all in the southeastern United States, adopted the Pentecostal message in direct response to the Azusa Street revival. To the doctrine of the second blessing of sanctification they tacked on a "third blessing," the Pentecostal baptism in the Spirit, marked by speaking in tongues. The holiness movement, apart from these southeastern groups, chose to reject the Pentecostal position. Two of the formative leaders in the holiness-Pentecostal movement were **Ambrose Jessup Tomlinson** (1865–1943) and **Charles Harrison Mason** (1866–1961).

At 24, when he narrowly escaped being struck by lightning, A. J. Tomlinson committed his life to Christ. In June 1903, Tomlinson, after what he reported to be a revelation from the Lord, identified with a small body of believers, called the Holiness Church, that had been formed the previous year by Richard Spurling and W. F. Bryant. He felt this to be a latter-day manifestation of the Apostolic

Church. Membership in this body was essential to salvation since God had revealed to him that this was now the one true church restored in the last days.

In January 1906, the federation of Holiness Churches held a general assembly, with Tomlinson serving as moderator and clerk. In 1907, the name Church of God was adopted. Each year Tomlinson served the fellowship as moderator. In 1914, he was unanimously made general overseer for life.

In 1908, G. B. Cashwell, who had come from the Los Angeles revival, preached at the general assembly of the Church of God, proclaiming the Pentecostal message. Tomlinson was already inclined this way, and the Church of God readily accepted the teaching, tacking on the Pentecostal experience as a third work of grace.

Tomlinson traveled widely, organizing churches. He launched the *Church of God Evangel*, serving as its editor, and in 1913 was instrumental in establishing a publishing house for the denomination. In addition to his other duties, he served in 1917 as superintendent of the Cleveland Bible Training School, the first school opened by the Church of God.

Without question, Tomlinson was a remarkable leader. But an unfortunate controversy marred his relationship with the Church of God council of elders in 1922. He was accused of financial wrongdoing, but was ultimately exonerated. He left the Church of God to form what eventually became known as the Church of God of Prophecy, with headquarters in Cleveland, Tennessee. Tomlinson served as general overseer of this splinter group until his death in 1943.

Charles Harrison Mason was the founder and long-time presiding bishop of the Church of God in Christ (COGIC), a very large and predominantly black Pentecostal body. He was born near Memphis, Tennessee, to newly freed slaves. When he was about fourteen, Charles was instantly healed of a serious affliction. He was baptized shortly afterward and began to work as a lay preacher in southern Arkansas. He was ordained in 1891 to the Baptist ministry in Preston, Arkansas.

Through the influence of Charles Price Jones, a black Baptist pastor from Jackson, Mississippi, Mason entered into the experience of sanctification. He and Jones taught this doctrine throughout several southern states, often splitting Baptist congregations. And in 1897, based on what Mason felt to be a revelation from God, he chose to bring into being a black denomination to be called the Church of God in Christ.

One of the earliest Pentecostal bodies to become legally incorporated, the COGIC issued credentials to people of all races. It is significant that many of the early white Pentecostal leaders were first ordained in this group. Until 1914, when the Assemblies of God came into existence, there were as many white COGIC congregations as there were black.

Until his death at ninety-five, Mason led the COGIC. Under his direction, the denomination grew to a membership of a half-million. And, in spite of the retreat of Pentecostalism to the practice of racial segregation, Mason maintained cordial relationships with his colleagues in the newly formed white Pentecostal denominations, and was highly respected by all Pentecostal leaders.

Stabilizing influences
From its beginnings, the Pentecostal movement, like revival movements before it, faced the problem of stability. The largest of the American Pentecostal bodies, the Assemblies of God, owes a considerable debt to several far-sighted leaders who established the principle that all theology, practice, and experience must be tested by the objective revelation of the Bible. They further insisted that the Pentecostal movement owed a large debt to the rich heritage of Christian history. Among those who shaped this pattern of stability were E. S. Williams, general superintendent from 1929 to 1949; educators P. C. Nelson, W. I. Evans, and Myer Pearlman; and Noel Perkin ("Mr. Missions"), who established the foundations for the largest of the Pentecostal missions organizations. Symbolizing the contributions of such men is the life of **Joseph Roswell Flower** (1888–1970).

Born in Canada, Flower was reared in a pious home. He was converted while studying law in Indianapolis in 1907. Two years later he received the Pentecostal baptism. This changed the course of his life. Ordained at a Pentecostal camp meeting in Plainfield, Indiana, Flower was soon engaged as pastor of a small flock in Indianapolis. It was here he began to publish the *Christian Evangel*, the first Pentecostal weekly paper and the forerunner of the *Pentecostal Evangel*, the weekly organ of the Assemblies of God. Flower, only twenty-six when the Assemblies' general council convened for the first time in April of 1914, was chosen to be general secretary, an office he held for a total of twenty-seven years (1914–16 and 1935–59). He would eventually serve in virtually every district office and national office except that of general superintendent.

At strategic points in the history of the Assemblies of God, the wisdom of Flower proved invaluable to the fledgling movement. Perhaps the most dramatic instance of his stablizing influence was his role in the "New Issue" controversy. In 1913, at a camp meeting in California, a "new revelation" teaching began that eventually led to a split in the American Pentecostal ranks, creating the entire subculture of oneness Pentecostalism. The newly formed Assemblies of God was especially hard hit. Many of the leaders, including the general chairman, E. N. Bell, were temporarily swept away by the enthusiasm. By 1915, the Assemblies of God was in grave peril. It was Flower who recognized, from his study of church history, that this "new revelation" was nothing other than a recurrence of the ancient heresy of Modal Monarchianism, or Sabellianism, an anti-Trinitiarian teaching that the Father, Son, and Spirit do not exist at the same time but as three successive modes of God. His steadying hand in an hour of near hysteria brought many of the leaders back into line and spared the Assemblies of God from possible disintegration.

Extraordinary evangelists
It is not incidental that evangelism and missions have been high on the agenda of Pentecostals from the beginning of the revival. In the early years, believers, upon being baptized in the Spirit, were expected to be immediately engaged in street meetings, house meetings, or other informal witnessing settings. Some "launched out in faith," moving from community to community in small "gospel bands."

A parade of outstanding Pentecostal revivalists could be listed, those whose itinerant ministries propelled frail congregations into thriving churches across North America and overseas. Charles S. Price, whose meetings in the Pacific Northwest in the 1920s through the 1940s were marked by great demonstrations of the power of God, is not atypical of that period. However, **Aimee Semple McPherson** (1890–1944) was easily the most colorful and successful of the early Pentecostal evangelists.

McPherson, founder of the International Church of the Foursquare Gospel, was born in Canada on a farm near Ingersoll, Ontario. In 1908, during meetings conducted in the town by Pentecostal evangelist Robert Semple, she made a commitment to Christ. She married the evangelist shortly thereafter, and they were both ordained a year later.

In 1910, the Semples went to China as missionaries. Only weeks after their arrival in Hong Kong for language study, Robert Semple contracted malaria and died, leaving a young widow not yet twenty years old. Upon her return to the United States, the young widow, now with a daughter, met Harold S. McPherson in New York. In 1911, they were married. However, the marriage ended in divorce ten years later.

McPherson established an effective itinerant ministry during these years. In city after city throughout Canada and the United States, her meetings, marked by evidences of God's power, frequently led denominational ministers into the "full-gospel" experience.

In 1921, she purchased property near Echo Park, a suburb of Los Angeles, for both a home and a church. Angelus Temple, seating more than five thousand, was dedicated two years later. In addition to writing and traveling to meetings, her efforts now entailed pastoring a church. Soon satellite churches began springing up, and in 1927 they were incorporated under the name of the International Church of the Foursquare Gospel.

Clothed in a flowing white gown, eloquent and personable, McPherson became a religious celebrity. Her dramatic sermons, her capacity to speak to the masses with feeling, and the diverse activities over which she presided, made her a public figure. Her radio station, KFSG, established in 1924, was one of the earliest attempts at gospel broadcasting. In 1923, L.I.F.E. Bible College was established. And well before the Depression, Angelus Temple captured the attention of the city for relief work among the poor.

In 1926, at the peak of her success, McPherson disappeared for a month. Resurfacing in Mexico, her tale of abduction made front-page news across the country. But charges that she had contrived the affair clouded her reputation. Nonetheless, the work she began continued. The ICFG developed a strong fellowship of churches, marked by a notable commitment to foreign missions. In spite of the sensationalism that seemed to surround Aimee McPherson, there is little question that she was responsible for leading more ministers into the Pentecostal fold than any single individual in the twentieth century.

Oral Granville Roberts (1918–), is without question the leading American healing evangelist of the recent past. Like many of the formative figures of Pentecostalism, Roberts was the product of rural poverty. He was reared in the home of a Holiness Pentecostal preacher in Oklahoma. When he was seventeen, he was instantly healed of tuberculosis and cured of stuttering. Shortly thereafter, young Roberts began his evangelistic ministry. He was ordained by the Holiness Pentecostal denomination in 1936.

In 1947, his itinerant healing ministry began with a citywide campaign in Enid, Oklahoma. He published his first book, started a monthly magazine, *Healing Waters* (renamed *Abundant Life* a decade later), and launched a regular radio broadcast—all in the same year. That year, too, he made Tulsa the headquarters of his evangelistic organization.

His 12,500-seat tent became a familiar sight in cities across the United States for many years. It was in this tent that his crusade style was developed, a pattern that shaped the ministries of hundreds of Pentecostal preachers. In 1955, Roberts launched a highly successful television program on which the nation could witness the remarkable healings that Roberts carefully documented with medical reports.

The most ambitious enterprises of his career were the opening of a major university in 1965, now worth a quarter of a billion dollars, and the more controversial City of Faith, a modern hospital and research center opened in 1981. Unlike some healing evangelists, Roberts has always maintained the propriety of medical science as a colleague in the healing ministry.

Although his luster may have dimmed in recent years, Roberts, with his positive proclamation, his remarkable faith, and his enormous vision, has earned a place of distinction among the leaders of American Pentecostalism.

"Mr. Pentecost"

In the early years of the revival, Pentecostals were spurned by fundamentalists and modernists alike. But in the mid-1950s, various denominations began to come to terms with the Pentecostal phenomenon. This re-evaluation came at the front end of the charismatic renewal, a movement that saw the New Testament gifts of the Spirit permitted, with some stipulations, within the major denominations. There were numerous bridge builders who reached across the ecclesiastical aisle to form relationships between Pentecostals and those in the larger church world. And the leading pioneer in this courageous ecumenical ministry was certainly **David Johannes du Plessis** (1905–87), "Mr. Pentecost."

Born of Huguenot parents in South Africa, du Plessis gave his heart to the Lord at age eleven after being frightened by a severe storm. He was baptized in the Apostolic Faith Mission, the Pentecostal denomination he served until his move to the United States and his identification with the Assemblies of God.

In December of 1936, British evangelist Smith-Wigglesworth, delivered to du Plessis a prophecy that was to change his ministry. The burden of the message was that du Plessis was to be a key to bringing the Pentecostal experience to the great denominations— and through this renewal would come an outpouring of blessing greater by far than the Pentecostal revival itself.

In 1947, du Plessis entered upon a new ministry. For the next decade he served as the organizing secretary for the World Pentecostal Conference (WPC), an activity that led him to move his family to the United States. He worked earnestly for the WPC since this was an ecumenical opportunity, a forum for Pentecostals of various nations and denominations to come together for fellowship. However, the Lord had larger plans for David du Plessis.

John Mackay, president of Princeton Seminary, invited du Plessis to the 1952 meeting of the International Missionary Council of the World Council of Churches (WCC) in Willingen, West Germany. He was asked to address the entire conference on the work of the Holy Spirit. From this initial contact, du Plessis began an ecumenical odyssey that would take him to prestigious ecclesiastical and academic centers. He encountered a deep hunger for the reality of God's presence nearly everywhere he went. His humility, his simple piety, and his joyful spirit captivated religious leaders in surprising places. The result was that hundreds of Christian statesmen from many lands were led by du Plessis into a deeper understanding of the person and work of the Holy Spirit. Doors began to open to Pentecostal values in an unprecedented way.

But there was a cost. Traditional Pentecostals did not know quite how to deal with the penetration of the Pentecostal experience into groups—such as the WCC—that had long been regarded as apostate. Evangelicals brought pressure to bear on the Assemblies of God, du Plessis' denomination, for the embarrassment he was causing evangelical Christianity. Good people did not associate with WCC types. The result was that du Plessis was defrocked by the Assemblies of God in 1962 for failure to desist from his ecumenical activities.

Happily, he was reinstated in 1980. By that time, many Pentecostal leaders had come to appreciate the unique and gifted ministry of this "Apostle of Love." His greatest achievement was the development of the Roman Catholic-Pentecostal Dialogue, a continuing series of meetings convened since Vatican II.

Without sacrificing the integrity of his own evangelical and Pentecostal convictions, the warmth and love of David du Plessis caused him to reach for ways to bring Christians together more effectively than any other Pentecostal of our time. Indeed, he saw in his later years the fulfillment of the prophecy given by Smith-Wigglesworth fifty years before his death. For du Plessis, the flow of the Spirit's refreshing, life-giving power was not to be limited to the Pentecostals alone. The Spirit has come to nourish all of God's church.

Azusa, a century later

I have attempted here to identify individuals who represent the formative generation of the Pentecostal movement. Today, that generation is almost entirely gone. The centennial of Azusa Street is now just a decade away. But in the footsteps of these unlikely leaders is a new generation of leaders ready to take the movement into the next century.

There are four areas in which younger Pentecostal leaders promise to make substantial contributions in the immediate future. First, in the arena of ecclesiastical leadership, the influence of pastors of large churches is noticeably increasing. In recent years in the

Assemblies of God, the denomination with which I am most conversant, Robert Schmidgall of Naperville, Illinois, and Glen Cole, of Sacramento, California, have been elected to the highest level of governance in the fellowship, the executive presbytery. Their churches are the largest in their respective districts. The denomination has evidently called for leadership to be closer to the front lines—that is, the successful local church.

Second, the Pentecostal movement has evolved rapidly with regard to the world of scholarship. Its roots were strongly marked by anti-intellectualism. As recently as midcentury, there were few college-bred people in positions of responsibility, either as pastors or even as teachers in the Bible colleges. Few of the early leaders were well educated. By the 1980s, however, the various strands within the movement could demonstrate considerable academic sophistication. In positions of academic influence, extending even beyond the periphery of Pentecostalism, are such names as Robert Cooley, president of Gordon-Conwell Divinity School, Gordon Fee of Regent College, Russell Spittler and Cecil Robeck of Fuller Theological Seminary, and Edith Blumhofer of Wheaton College. Within the Pentecostal movement, numerous colleges and at least two respectable seminaries are manned by well-trained staff. Large numbers of young Pentecostals are not only graduating from college, but a rapidly increasing number of prospective pastors are setting their sights on seminary and graduate studies as preparation for ministry.

Third, the Pentecostal movement has attracted considerable attention to its strong church growth, especially in areas outside the United States such as Latin America. As the early missionary pioneers have passed from the scene, younger leaders have surfaced. George Flattery of Brussels has been the innovator of the world-girdling ministry known as the International Correspondence Institute. And Loren Triplett has surfaced as a strategic and imaginative leader for the Assemblies of God in its huge Latin American outreach (there are an estimated seven million adherents in Brazil alone).

Fourth, in the arena of interchurch relations, younger statesmen are surfacing within the ranks of the Pentecostals. The charismatic renewal generated new tensions for Pentecostals, for this unusual awakening pressed upon existing Pentecostal leadership a challenge for which most did not seem well-prepared. How do you relate to those claiming gifts of the Spirit, but who belong to traditions long held suspect by evangelicals and Pentecostals?

It remains to be seen, in the next generation, which individuals will rise to fill the role of such statesmen as David du Plessis. Vinson Synan of the Pentecostal Holiness denomination is perhaps the most articulate and able statesman of the younger generation representing American Pentecostalism to the larger church world. Demanded of the statesmen of the next decade will be the task of aiding the Pentecostal movement to retain those values that give it useful identity and, at the same time, of building the proper kind of bridges with the larger horizons of Christianity.

Chapter 3

AN EQUAL OPPORTUNITY MOVEMENT

Vinson Synan

As Grant Wacker noted in the opening chapter, Pentecostals come in a "bewildering variety." And one prominent sub-group that has played a pivotal role in the movement from its very beginnings is America's black population. Indeed, black Pentecostalism represents an indigenous form of American Christianity that has affected not only the United States, but the entire Christian world.

Preparing for "Pentecost"
The post–Civil War holiness movement in America had its beginnings in 1867 with the founding of the National Holiness Association in New Jersey. Although begun by Methodists, the movement soon spread to most Protestant church bodies, both black and white.

Two major black holiness churches that later became part of the Pentecostal movement were formed at this time. These were the United Holy Church (UHC), founded by Henry L. Fisher in 1886, and the Church of God in Christ (COGIC), founded in 1897 by Charles Harrison Mason and Charles Price Jones. Although the founders of both groups had been Baptists, they accepted the Wesleyan teaching on sanctification as a second work of grace and started their churches as perfectionistic "holiness" churches.[1]

In the beginning, these groups differed little from the Church of the Nazarene and other Wesleyan denominations, emphasizing a strict code of outward holiness. However, a revolutionary change came to these groups in the period 1906–09 through the ministry of black leader William Joseph Seymour, pastor of the storied Azusa Street Mission in Los Angeles.

Azusa Street and Holy Ghost baptism

When Pentecostalism appeared in 1901, it was led by a white man, Charles Fox Parham, a former Methodist from Topeka, Kansas. Parham insisted on speaking in tongues as the "initial evidence" of the baptism in the Holy Spirit. This position on tongues became a distinguishing hallmark of the movement. However, Parham's leadership in the movement waned after 1907, precisely at a time when blacks came to leadership under Seymour at Azusa Street.

Almost from the beginning, the Pentecostal movement caused division and realignment among blacks as it did among whites. The most notable schism occurred in the COGIC, a church destined to become one of the largest Pentecostal churches in the world.

At the insistence of Charles Jones, Charles Mason and two other ministers visited Azusa Street in 1907 to investigate the revival. While there they received the tongues-attested baptism and returned to Memphis as confirmed Pentecostals. Jones, however, refused to accept the Pentecostal experience and opposed its spread in the church. After a period of debate, a schism ensued with Mason leading the Pentecostal contingent, which maintained the legally chartered name "Church of God in Christ." Jones's group eventually adopted the name "Church of Christ (Holiness)."[2]

Mason's church soon attracted many white ministers due to the fact that the COGIC was the only legally chartered Pentecostal denomination in the nation (and with legal recognition came lower clergy rates on the railroads). The racial tables were now turned as Mason ordained whites and signed their ordination papers. What made this more incredible was the fact that it occurred in the South during the most racist period of Jim Crow segregation.[3]

In time the ties between Mason and the white ministers became more tenuous, however, with little direct connection between church officials and the white ministers. In a "gentleman's agreement," whites were given the right to issue credentials in Mason's name with the understanding that "unworthy" candidates would not be ordained.[4]

Divided by oneness

After 1911, the Pentecostal movement was torn by a new issue that divided the newly formed Assemblies of God (established in 1914). Known as the "oneness" movement, and pejoratively as the "Jesus Only" movement, it taught a modalism that saw Jesus Christ as both Father and Holy Spirit, as well as the Son of God. Added to this rejection of the Trinity was an insistence that water baptism "in Jesus' name" was the only scriptural mode, and that this was valid only when the newly baptized spoke in other tongues.[5]

One of the few blacks to join the Assemblies of God in 1914 was Garfield T. Haywood of Indianapolis, whose congregation was one of the denomination's largest. To the consternation of church officials, he and his congregation were swept into the oneness movement in 1915. Haywood subsequently helped form the Pentecostal Assemblies of the World (PAW), which began as a racially integrated church body with roughly equal numbers of black and white members.[6]

By 1924, the whites separated from the main body of the PAW and formed groups that resulted in the organization of the United Pentecostal Church (UPC) in 1945. A practically all-white body, the UPC became the largest Oneness church, while the PAW continued its attempts at running a racially integrated church. Racial equality was institutionalized in the PAW by the adoption of a polity whereby blacks and whites would alternate in the position of presiding bishop.

Other Pentecostal groups reacted differently to the race problem.

In 1908 and 1913, blacks related to the Fire-Baptized Holiness and Pentecostal Holiness Church requested and were granted separate status. The Church of God (Cleveland, Tenn.) was unique in that it maintained its black congregations as part of the mainstream of the church. Many of the black Churches of God were founded by Edmund Barr, who was commissioned by A. J. Tomlinson to evangelize among blacks.

When a major schism in the Church of God occurred in 1923 over the leadership of Tomlinson, a new church resulted, which eventually took the name "Church of God of Prophecy" (COGOP). This church successfully maintained a large contingency of black members, both in the United States and in the Caribbean Islands. Today it is one of the most fully integrated denominations in America.[7]

Contributions of black Pentecostalism
Not surprisingly, black Pentecostals have continued to play a critical role in the area of race relations. For example, they played an important—if quiet—part in the civil-rights movement. Like the National Baptist Convention, the Church of God in Christ did not openly endorse the movement. Nevertheless, individual clergymen did participate in local demonstrations. Among these were Arthur Brazier in Chicago, Ithiel Clemmons and Bishop Frederick Washington in New York, Talbert Swan in Massachusetts, and Levi Willis in Virginia.[8]

There was also the tacit support from black Pentecostal leaders that the public did not always see. For example, on the night before his assassination, Martin Luther King, Jr., made his famous "mountaintop" speech from the podium of Mason Temple in Memphis, the headquarters of the COGIC. In fact, the garbage workers' strike that occasioned King's fateful visit to Memphis was organized by members of the COGIC under the leadership of Bishop J. O. Patterson.[9]

The advent of liberation theology in the 1970s found vocal support among some black Pentecostal leaders who saw a persistent racism within the American movement. This charge was often coupled with an attempt to upgrade the position of Seymour vis à vis Parham as the founding father of the Pentecostal movement. Leading voices in this school of thought were Leonard Lovett, who served as dean of the C. H. Mason Theological Seminary in Atlanta, and James Tinney, publisher of a black Pentecostal scholarly journal, *Spirit.*[10]

Black Pentecostals and the charismatic movement

When the charismatic renewal movement entered the mainline churches after 1960, black involvement (and consequently, black influence) was almost nonexistent. There were, however, several mainline leaders who took an open and active part in the movement. Taking the lead in the African Methodist Episcopal church were Bishop Vernon Byrd, a missionary to Africa, and John Bryant, pastor of the Bethel AME Church in Baltimore. Leaders of the movement in the Church of God (Anderson, Ind.) were Benjamin Reed and Milton Granum.[11]

A sign of an increasing desire to bridge the charismatic racial gap was the introduction of a new magazine in 1987 entitled *Bridgebuilders*. Published by Evangel Temple, a large black congregation in Washington, D.C., pastored by John Meares, a white pastor with roots in the Church of God (Cleveland, Tenn.), this bimonthly periodical describes itself as "the Christian magazine committed to racial unity in the church." According to Meares, there has never been a true reconciliation between blacks and whites since the Civil War. His purpose is to bring about that reconciliation through the Pentecostal/charismatic movement.[12]

Indeed, by the end of the 1980s there were signs of major charismatic and ecumenical breakthroughs into the black Christian community. Such black preachers as Ben Kinchloe, Carlton Pearson, and Frederick Price became televangelists of national influence commanding the allegiance of millions of whites as well as blacks.

Opportunities in the next century

As the century moves toward its close, the Pentecostal movement has become an equal-opportunity movement, especially for blacks entering the ministry. The huge growth of the movement has meant the opening of thousands of pulpits for aspiring young black preachers. According to research done by Charles Jones in his volume *Black Holiness*, the size of the movement among blacks in America in 1982 was:[13]

Black Holiness-Pentecostal Movement

Churches	Members	Ministers
13,413	4,071,289	39,592

Black Finished-work Pentecostal Movement

Churches	Members	Ministers
372	46,500	868

Black Oneness–Pentecostal Movement

Churches	Members	Ministers
3,951	788,541	10,996

Totals

17,736	4,906,330	51,456

In addition to these figures for North America, researcher David Barrett estimates there are no less than 42,128,880 denominational Pentecostals in Africa, most of whom are black. By adding this figure to the totals of black Pentecostals in North and South America, the number may easily approach 100 million persons.[14] And of these, an estimated 300 thousand blacks are ministering full-time in the worldwide Pentecostal/charismatic movement.[15]

This indicates that the Pentecostal movement has provided great opportunities for full-time ministry for blacks all over the world. And with William J. Seymour and Azusa Street as models, the prospects for even more staggering growth in the future are exceedingly bright.

Notes

1. C. H. Mason, *History and Formative Years of the Church of God in Christ with Excerpts from the Life and Works of Its Founder: Bishop C. H. Mason* (Memphis: Church of God in Christ Publishing House, 1973); Henry Lee Fisher, *The History of the United Holy Church of America, Inc.* (Durham, N.C.: 1974), pp. 43–95.

2. For a sympathetic account of black Pentecostalism, see Walter Hollenweger's *The Pentecostals: The Charismatic Movement in the*

Churches (Minneapolis: Augsburg Publishing House, 1972), pp. 1–74; Synan, *Holiness-Pentecostal Movement* (Grand Rapids, Mich.: Wm. B. Eerdmans, 1971), pp. 165–84. Also see James Tinney, "Black Origins of the Pentecostal Movement," *Christianity Today*, Vol. 16, No.1, October 8, 1971, pp. 4–6.

3. Robert Mapes Anderson, *Vision of the Disinherited*, (New York: Oxford University Press, 1979) pp. 140–89.

4. C. F. Range, *et al.*, *Church of God in Christ: Official Manual* (Memphis: Church of God in Christ Publishing House, 1973), pp. XXIII–XXXVII; Anderson, *Vision of the Disinherited*, pp. 176–94.

5. David D. Reed, "Aspects of the Origins of Oneness Pentecostalism," in Vinson Synan, *Aspects of Pentecostal-Charismatic Origins* (Plainfield, N.J.: Logos International, 1974), pp. 143–68.

6. Morris Golder, *History of the Pentecostal Assemblies of the World* (Indianapolis, 1973).

7. Charles W. Conn, *Like a Mighty Army: A History of the Church of God, 1886–1976*, rev. ed. (Cleveland, Tenn.: Pathway Press, 1977), pp. 132–353.

8. David Daniels, personal interview with the author, December 15, 1988; Ithiel Clemmons, personal interview with the author, December 19, 1988.

9. Gayraud Wilmore, *Last Things First* (Philadelphia: Westminster Press, 1982), pp. 88–9.

10. *Spirit* was published from 1977 to 1979 in Washington, D.C. Tinney later espoused the gay-rights cause as a problem for Pentecostals. He died in 1988 from AIDS-related causes.

11. See John Meares, "Why the White Church Needs to Repent for Black Slavery." *Bridgebuilder: The Christian Magazine Committed to Racial Unity in the Church*, March/April, 1987, p. 7. Meares teaches that the civil-rights movement was a "work of the Holy Spirit" that should be praised by Pentecostals.

12. Ithiel Clemmons, "The Voice of the Black Church in New Orleans Rings Loud, Clear." *AD2000 Together*, pp. 8–9.

13. Charles E. Jones, *Black Holiness: A Guide to the Study of Black Participation in Wesleyan Perfectionistic and Glossolalic Pentecostal Movements* (Metuchen, N.J.: The Scarecrow Press, 1987), passim.

14. David Barrett, "The Twentieth Century Pentecostal/Charismatic Renewal in the Holy Spirit, with Its Goal of World Evangeli-

zation," presented in the *International Bulletin of Missionary Research* (1988); in *AD2000 Together*, Fall, 1988, pp. 11–12; and in Stanley M. Burgess, *et. al.*, *Dictionary of Pentecostal and Charismatic Movements* (Grand Rapids, Mich.: Zondervan Publishing House, 1988), pp. 810–30.

15. Barrett, ibid.

AMERICA'S PENTECOSTALS: WHAT THEY BELIEVE

Chapter 4

PENTECOSTALS BELIEVE IN MORE THAN TONGUES

Gordon L. Anderson

T he Pentecostal movement is known for its emphasis on the baptism of the Holy Spirit and the practice of speaking in unknown tongues.* That a movement is known by its central emphasis is understandable, but Pentecostal doctrine is much more than a single issue. What, then, do Pentecostals and charismatics believe?

This is not an easy question to answer. The Pentecostal movement is made up of many different groups, each with its own special set of

---

*The author is indebted to three works on the Pentecostal movement. They are: Burgess, Stanley M., and McGee, Gary B. *Dictionary of Pentecostal and Charismatic Movements*. Grand Rapids, Michigan: Regency Reference Library (Zondervan) 1988; Hollenweger, Walter J. *The Pentecostals*. Peabody, Massachusetts: Hendrickson Publishers, 1988, first published in 1972; Menzies, William W. *Anointed to Serve*. Springfield, Missouri: Gospel Publishing House, 1971.

emphases. It is impossible to pinpoint what they all believe on everything. Nonetheless, Pentecostals do have a number of common characteristics along with a shared core of biblical doctrine.

Who is a Pentecostal?

The term "Classical Pentecostals" refers to those who identify with traditional Pentecostal groups, beliefs, and practices, including the more traditional Pentecostal worship forms. The roots for this group are in the 1901–06 Pentecostal revival. Charismatics, on the other hand, identify with a newer renewal begun in 1960. Among its characteristics are the singing of choruses based on Scripture and vigorous worship, which occasionally includes dancing or hand waving. Since these differences are not doctrinally substantive, all those who espouse a doctrine of the baptism of the Holy Spirit can be called Pentecostals.*

Great emphasis is placed on the experiential side of the Christian life among Pentecostals. And they have shown themselves to be uniquely adept at adding the Pentecostal experience to almost any theological school of thought—even those that seem least able to accommodate it. For example, John Calvin proclaimed the cessation of visible gifts, but there are some Pentecostal Calvinists. And while dispensationalists relegate miraculous signs and wonders to the apostolic age, there are many Pentecostal dispensationalists. Thus Pentecostals believe that any Christian, regardless of his or her theological position, may experience the Pentecostal blessing. This accounts for the variety found in the Pentecostal movement.

There are, however, at least two beliefs holding all Pentecostals together. These are: (1) a commitment to the inspiration and authority of Scripture, and (2) a doctrine of the experiential nature of the believer's relationship with God. This later doctrine asserts that God is personal and that he is known and experienced personally. For the Pentecostal there are two important spiritual experiences. The first is the New Birth. The second is the teaching of the baptism of the Holy Spirit.

---

*For the purposes of this chapter the term *Pentecostal* refers to all those who espouse the doctrine of the baptism of the Holy Spirit and speaking in tongues. Individual subgroups are identified when necessary.

The core of belief

Thus Pentecostals and charismatics share a doctrinal core with mainline evangelical Christians. They believe in the inspiration and authority of Scripture. They share the doctrine of the primacy of the Word with all those movements that were spawned by the Reformation. It is the recognition of this core that has prompted key evangelical leaders such as Carl F. H. Henry and the late Harold J. Ockenga to maintain fellowship with the Pentecostal community in spite of the differences that might divide them.

Pentecostals and charismatics also believe in the necessity of a born-again experience of salvation and all the supporting doctrines that go with it (sin, confession, repentance, faith, forgiveness, justification, etc.). In addition, they believe in water baptism, the need for a holy life, local-church involvement (the priesthood of the believer), evangelism and missions, and the reality of heaven and hell.

Pentecostals do, however, have unique characteristics that have to do more with attitudes, commitments, and practices than with the fundamentals of doctrine. These characteristics are important and are a large part of the unique identity of Pentecostals.

First, most Pentecostals, especially the classical groups, are not creedal and theological movements. Experiences with God provide a basis for their faith. They produce statements of faith that outline basic doctrinal commitments, but they do not tool out comprehensive creeds or systematic theologies. This is intentional; Pentecostals believe that tight creeds can be divisive and that they can unduly restrict the understanding and experience of God. They celebrate the fact that revivals bring a fresh understanding of the Word of God and that this often has the effect of unsettling older established creeds that have painted God into a theological box. They also believe that systematic theology can be comprehended intellectually but not lived out experientially, a situation Pentecostals abhor.

This same tendency can be recognized among the mainline denominational charismatics. They tolerate a certain degree of tension between their traditional doctrines and practices and their new-found beliefs. It is not that they take doctrine lightly. It is just that they are committed to maintaining a lively relationship with God and to avoiding the paralyzing effects of theological arguments.

Second, Pentecostals are emotional. They have rediscovered that the emotional life is a part of God's created order and that it is a powerful engine for action. The power of these emotions can be seen in giving, missions, worship, and witnessing. These are positive expressions of the emotional side of life. However, not all the Pentecostal emphasis on emotion is healthy. Responding with an undue dependence on the emotions can result in the uncritical acceptance of leaders, doctrines, and practices that should be rejected.

Typically older and more stable Pentecostal churches deemphasize emotions because of the excesses that have characterized some expressions of Pentecostal faith. In doing so, however, some have paralyzed the zeal that has been one of the salutary contributions of the Pentecostal movement. Happily, many more have brought a healthy and needed balance to this zeal. Age and experience can bring much-needed maturity.

Third, Pentecostals emphasize the personal knowledge of God and expect an existential encounter with a God whose presence can be felt and experienced. They desire religious experiences that are "better felt than telt, better walked than talked." Cathartic conversions and rededications, baptisms, deliverances, healings, calls into ministry, and the like, are commonplace. Pentecostals exhibit a familiar, even casual, approach to the matter of God's presence.

Fourth, Pentecostals tend to favor action over contemplation and study. They want to "do" something for God, not just learn more about him. While this is more true of the older, traditional Pentcostals than it is of the newer charismatics, still, both expressions of Pentecostal faith are action-oriented. For the most part, Pentecostals build discipleship training centers, institutes, and Bible colleges rather than graduate schools and seminaries. The need to get people out into ministry as soon as possible is felt deeply.

Finally, Pentecostals are resistant to organization and centralized authority, preferring the freedom to act on their own understanding of the will of God. This follows from a belief that the Holy Spirit, not denominations, leads people, and that the prophet has always been in opposition to the religious establishment, not a product of it. As may be expected, this has had both good and bad consequences. It has given great men and women of God the latitude needed to exercise their ministries fully, resulting in noteworthy achievements. It has also allowed others enough rope to hang themselves and embarrass their colleagues in the process.

A commitment to Scripture
In addition to this basic core of evangelical faith to which Pentecostals subscribe, there are other doctrines critical to the makeup of the Pentecostal believer.

First among Pentecostal teachings is a deep commitment to the inspiration of Scriptures. The statements of faith produced by Pentecostal denominations are uniform in their articulation of a conservative understanding of the Word of God. And charismatics who are part of denominations which have historically taken a more liberal approach to the Bible tend to become more conservative when they accept Pentecostal teachings.

The primary reason for this conservatism is that the Pentecostal understanding of the experiences in the Bible (the New Birth, the baptism of the Holy Spirit, speaking in tongues, miracles, and the operation of the gifts of the Spirit) are more subject to deletion or reinterpretation by liberal interpreters than are other doctrines. Liberals are not known for their desire to retain the miraculous or the unusual doctrines and practices that show up in Scriptures. Since Pentecostals and charismatics believe in these things, a more literalistic view of Scripture usually accompanies the Pentecostal experience.

Pentecostals believe that the Bible, correctly interpreted, is the authoritative guide to faith and practice. Current conservative evangelical standards for the interpretation of the Bible are accepted. The historical/grammatical method and the search for the intended meaning of the author to the original audience are commonplace.

Pentecostals use both the propositional passages and the historical passages to establish doctrine. This has been a hotly debated issue among Pentecostals, as it has among other groups. But the importance of this discussion is acutely felt by Pentecostals who place great weight on historical narratives as the basis for doctrine, like speaking in tongues. Some even go so far as to make the narratives determinative when an apparent conflict appears between a propositional passage and a historical narrative. Some see the narratives as prescriptive models to be imitated. The problem with this approach, of course, is that everything the early church did is not necessarily a model for the modern church.

Pentecostals are aware of this problem and seek to avoid the kinds of excesses that such an approach to Scripture can produce. However, once one has adopted a hermeneutic that sees the historical narratives as normative, one has difficulty determining which biblical models are excessive and which ones are acceptable.

Another important facet of Pentecostal hermeneutics is the use of allegorization. While the practice of using allegorization is definitely not endorsed by the majority of Pentecostals, there is a functional acceptance of the preaching and teaching of allegorized narratives, parables, and so on along with other imaginative interpretations. In some quarters, for example, the practice has reached such exaggerated proportions that every nut and bolt, every hide and hair in the tabernacle stands for some spiritual principle in the church. This is probably one of the more serious problems Pentecostals face with regard to Bible interpretation.

One of the strengths of Pentecostalism is its emphasis on personal, existential experiences with God. Pentecostals are not unnerved by the search for a theological explanation for a divine act that has been experienced but not understood. Using this approach, the search cannot help using historical and personal supernatural experiences as a part of the formulation of doctrine. This is in contrast to groups that discount anything for which their doctrine has no explanation.

The matter of tongues

A second important doctrine that is uniquely Pentecostal is that of the baptism of the Holy Spirit and speaking in tongues. This doctrine has roots in the Wesleyan teaching of the second blessing of sanctification, which they believed purifies the life from sin. Pentecostals adopted the idea that there is a second blessing that follows salvation, but they added that it imparts spiritual power for ministry along with the ability to speak in tongues. In addition, they believe that the baptism makes one able to function in the other gifts of the Spirit that are outlined in 1 Corinthians 12. Except for a few in the minority fringe, Pentecostals do not believe that the baptism of the Holy Spirit is necessary for salvation.

The doctrine of the baptism of the Holy Spirit is the single most distinctive teaching of Pentecostals. There have, however, been differences of opinion on some of the details of its operation. When the Pentecostal revival broke out at the beginning of this century, opinion was uniform that the baptism of the Holy Spirit was primarily an enduement of power for ministry. Taking Acts 1:8 as the key text for this understanding, Pentecostals believed that the Spirit was given to the early church so that it could effectively evangelize the world. It is not surprising then to find that early Pentecostals had an ardent desire to evangelize the world and that missions activity was a priority when the various Pentecostal groups began to organize. That the baptism is primarily for the bestowal of power was uniformly held by Pentecostals until the 1960s and the emergence of the charismatic renewal.

The new charismatics did not abandon the idea that the Pentecostal baptism brought a gift of power, but they did add another dimension that altered the understanding that its primary purpose was power for ministry. Charismatics emphasized that speaking in tongues was a prayer language that enabled one to communicate directly with God without the interference of the human intellect and the vehicle of a known language. The purpose of this communication is personal edification. The key verse for this position is 1 Corinthians 14:2, which indicates that one who speaks in an unknown tongue edifies himself. Therefore, with the heavy emphasis on the personal nature of the power of the Holy Spirit, it comes as no surprise that some charismatics have not shown the same degree of missions fervor as older Pentecostals.

A second understanding of the purpose of speaking in unknown tongues is that it edifies the church if it occurs in a public service and is accompanied by an interpretation. The interpretation functions as does the gift of prophecy and is used to build up the body of Christ. Pentecostals believe that all those who are baptized in the Holy Spirit speak in tongues, but that only a few are used to give public messages. This is how they understand the indication of 1 Corinthians 12:29–30 that all do not speak with tongues.

The third purpose of speaking in tongues is that it is a miraculous sign to unbelievers. This happens when people speak a human language they have never learned (not an unknown tongue) in the presence of those who know that language. This is what happened in Acts 2:8. Pentecostals give testimony of this miracle taking place from time to time. In his book *The Pentecostals*, Walter J. Hollenweger recounts the story of a Jewish rabbi who attended an Assemblies of God service in Pasadena, Texas, in 1960. During the service he heard a man speaking perfect Hebrew. The man had never studied a word of Hebrew in his life.

Pentecostals have traditionally held that speaking in tongues is the initial physical evidence of the baptism of the Holy Spirit. While this is the majority opinion, this teaching has not always gone uncontested. In the early years of the Pentecostal revival, F. F. Bosworth, a respected Pentecostal leader, began to assert that any one of the gifts of the Spirit spoken of in 1 Corinthians 12:8–10 could serve as a sign of the baptism. While his opinion has not prevailed among classical Pentecostals, it has experienced renewed support among some charismatics. A significant number of people in the charismatic renewal do not speak in tongues and never expect to do so.

Divine healing and end-times thinking

The third distinguishing Pentecostal doctrine is divine healing. Pentecostals believe in the current operation of the gifts of the Spirit as outlined in 1 Corinthians 12:8–10, and they believe that the baptism of the Holy Spirit provides the ability to function in these gifts. Therefore, Pentecostal churches regularly pray for the sick or invite the sick to have the church elders pray and lay hands on them. This practice is taken from the biblical injunction of James 5:14.

Healing evangelists and revivals that emphasize the miraculous have been prevalent throughout the history of the Pentecostal movement. Some of these individuals have earned bad reputations because of personal failures and the inappropriate sensationalism they produced in their public ministries, even to the point of faking miracles to "prime the pump" of faith. These, however, constitute a highly visible but very small minority of Pentecostal ministries. They pale in comparison to the number of Pentecostals who have taught and practiced a doctrine of the miraculous without compromising the character of their personal lives or their ministries.

Pentecostals have, for the most part, handled the doctrine of divine healing with care. They believe that God heals, but they also understand that healing is not always possible. The miraculous is a mystery. Pentecostals recognize that there are many factors in the issue of sickness and healing and that the power of God cannot be manipulated to guarantee 100 percent results. They believe in doctors and medicine and do not believe that their use indicates a lack of faith in God.

There is one group of Pentcostals, however, that has pushed the doctrine of healing beyond what is warranted by Scripture. The Faith/Word movement takes the position that both salvation and healing are provided in the Atonement and that one must only have faith to appropriate them both. If people have enough faith they can be saved. Likewise, if they have enough faith they can be healed. There are no other mitigating factors. They even go so far as to declare that worldly prosperity is a promise of God and that faith will secure it as well.

It seems that the excesses of this movement have peaked and that much-needed correction to the simplistic logic and exegesis supporting the position has been offered by its leaders. Still, there is a sizable number of churches and leaders that are distinctive because of this doctrine. It is to be hoped that, in time, these Pentecostals will work through the difficulties of their position and come to the consensus that is much like the one tooled out by traditional Pentecostals who dealt with the same excesses, but in an earlier generation.

The fourth major doctrine that is important to Pentecostals is their eschatalogical position. Rather, one should say, positions, since there is so much variety and so little agreement. The eschatatology of Pentecostals is important because it has generated a great deal of emotion and motivation for their other activities.

Until recently, the one point on which Pentecostals have had the most agreement has been on the doctrine of the imminent return of the Lord Jesus Christ. Emotional messages on the rapture of the church and the second coming of the Lord have punctuated the ministries of many Pentecostal preachers. But now there are growing differences of opinion on this doctrine.

The Restoration movement, which emerged in the late 1940s, holds a premillennial, posttribulation position, believing that the tribulation spoken of in Daniel was fulfilled in the Jews in the first century. They do not look for a tribulation prior to the second coming, but neither do they emphasize the immediacy of that event either. They have an optimistic view of the role of the church in the world and believe that the church should expend its energy extending the kingdom rather than preaching a rescue-mission Rapture or Second Coming.

Another group, the Kingdom Now movement, takes a postmillennial position. For these Pentecostals, the Second Coming might be a thousand years away. The important thing for them is to establish the millennial kingdom in the here and now so that Jesus can return. This movement, with its positive approach to the establishment of the kingdom and its "dominion mentality," has been attractive to the newer charismatics as well as to some of the older traditional Pentecostals.

Among more traditional Pentecostals there is a mixture of pre- and posttribulation premillennialism, as well as some amillennialism. This observation underscores the fact that the significance of eschatology for the Pentecostal rests not in the extent to which the different groups agree, but on the impetus that eschatological concerns has provided for the different groups.

Fighting demonic powers

The final distinctive Pentecostal doctrine that deserves attention is demonology. Pentecostals understand that the kingdom of God includes power over demons. They recognize that the Cross and Resurrection secured the victory over Satan, but they tend to emphasize that the baptism of the Holy Spirit gives a person power to cast out demons in the same way Jesus did.

From time to time, revivals of Pentecostal power have included an emphasis on demon possession and the power of the believer over the satanic realm. The Latter Rain revival of 1948–53 brought a renewal of attention to the demonic. Not all of this was good, of course. A few Pentecostal ministries sensationalized the issue all out of proportion. But as has been the case throughout the history of Pentecost, the claim that believers have power over demons was unapologetically proclaimed.

It is most interesting to note that the charismatic renewal has brought with it another emphasis on demons. In fact, it is rather astonishing that some in this renewal have introduced the idea that even Christians can be demon possessed. Some of the mainline denominational charismatics regularly practice exorcisms, and one charismatic Lutheran church has a minister on staff who specializes in casting demons out of Christians. The extreme fringe who hold this belief have gone so far as to attribute almost any difficulty Christians experience to demonic control. Some of it is so ludicrous that it is funny (a demon of fingernail biting, for example), but other expressions of it are tragic (attributing sickness and death to demonic activity and lack of faith and power on the part of the believer).

The teaching that Christians can be demon possessed has met with strong opposition from most traditional Pentecostals. Older Pentecostals have believed that nonbelievers can be possessed, but they have ardently resisted the idea that a born-again believer can be under demonic control.

Part of the success that Pentecostals have had in missions is based on their willingness to deal boldly with demon possessions and related phenomena. Many cultures in the world believe in spiritual forces, powers, ghosts, spells, curses, and other similar manifestations of the demonic realm. Pentecostal missionaries have attacked these spiritual forces with ministries and demonstrations that have been convincing to the local populace, bringing them to faith in Christ.

In the Western world we are not accustomed to overt encounters with demonic power and thus take a skeptical approach to alleged demonic demonstrations. Some denominations do not believe in demon possession and attribute to various psychological disorders the strange behavior that people in foreign lands believe to be caused by demons. Yet Pentecostal missionaries have shown themselves quite ready to accept the reality of the manifestations of demonic activity and to challenge the power of those demons with the power of Christ.

Summary

On the one hand, Pentecostals are different from other members of the body of Christ in many ways. On the other hand, it should be remembered that the stereotyped image of a Pentecostal can be the result of a few highly publicized oddities rather than fundamental differences in belief. The attempt here has been to show those points at which Pentecostals identify with the evangelical community. The similarities are numerous and significant.

Pentecostals believe in a great deal more than speaking in tongues. Those differences in emphasis and doctrine that do exist can be seen in the broader context of the unique contribution that Pentecostals have made to the body of Christ.

Chapter 5

QUESTIONS OF HEALTH AND WEALTH

James R. Goff, Jr.

N othing has prompted more debate within Pentecostal and charismatic circles over the last decade than the controversy over faith healing and Christian prosperity. Nicknamed by detractors as the "health-and-wealth" or "name it–claim it" gospel, the "word-of-faith" movement* has successfully captured a vocal segment of the growing charismatic revival.[1] Though the specific number of adherents is not known, it features some of the charismatic movement's most powerful evangelists and largest multimedia ministries. The battlefield that has developed in the wake of this growth has threatened both the identity and the unity of the twentieth-century charismatic renewal.

---

*I am using the term *faith movement* because it is neither pejorative nor patronizing.

Heal the sick

In short, the faith movement teaches that divine health and prosperity are the rights of every Christian who will appropriate enough faith to receive them. And the secret to appropriating such faith comes in making a positive confession and avoiding all doubt that the prayer of faith has been answered. In some ways, these ideas are only variations of themes that have been persistent in Pentecostal circles since the outbreak of the revival at the turn of the twentieth century. In other ways, the themes are unique and new.[2]

Pentecostals have long heralded divine healing as a cardinal doctrine. Indeed, divine healing was an important part of the nineteenth-century holiness movement that gave rise to one of the central wings of the early Pentecostal revival. As a result of the amorphous holiness movement, denominations as diverse as Episcopal and Baptist incorporated evangelists who championed the cause of healing by faith. The evangelical revivalist, educator, and reformer Charles Grandison Finney was himself an avid supporter. Critics charged that Finney's position on the availability of divine healing removed the mystery from religion by making God's will subject to human prayer. Unperturbed, Finney continued to argue that if a Christian "prays for a definite object," "prays in faith," and "expects to obtain the blessing," then "faith always obtains the object."[3]

By the late nineteenth century, healing had become an integral part of the theology of many who frequented holiness meetings. The healing ministries of Episcopalians Charles Cullis and Carrie Judd Montgomery, Presbyterian Albert Benjamin Simpson, and Baptist Adoniram Judson Gordon proclaimed that in the atonement of Jesus Christ, God had provided a way of dealing with the everyday struggles with health that most Americans faced.

Equally important was the impact of independent evangelist John Alexander Dowie, who broadcast the doctrine to the masses. Flamboyant and strongly authoritarian, the Australian faith healer preached an extreme form of the healing message that others before him had avoided. Located in Chicago in the 1890s, he turned his services into a religious sideshow, advertising authentic healings as always instantaneous and utterly denouncing the use of doctors and medicines.[4]

Early Pentecostals were influenced by the mainstream theology of leaders like A. J. Gordon and A. B. Simpson; at the same time, they were intrigued with the charm and apparent success of itinerants like Dowie. Though Dowie was himself an outspoken opponent of the Pentecostal revival, his uncompromising denunciation of the sin of "worldliness" placed him well within their understanding of inspired preaching. While Dowie seemed dangerous to many in the mainstream of the healing movement, he came across as an uncompromising prophet to the bulk of the outcast Pentecostals who formed separate denominations from their holiness brethren during the first two decades of the twentieth century. The message they adopted was thus one of radical faith in God to heal their diseases without benefit of man or man-made medicines. Not coincidental to the rise of Pentecostalism was the decline of healing theology among mainstream evangelicals. The excess of independents like Dowie and the desire to separate themselves from the disreputable Pentecostals forced most to stay away from any emphasis on healing within their circles.[5]

Getting rid of the Devil

All Pentecostal denominations included divine healing in the theological arsenal that they interpreted as setting the stage for Christ's second coming. Healing was one of the signs, along with the baptism of the Holy Spirit evidenced by speaking in tongues, that represented a descent of power on the last generation. The signs and wonders that would be wrought by this newfound power, they believed, would warrant the eruption of an end-time revival to win the lost and prepare the world for the end of the present age.[6]

As has already been described, Charles Fox Parham was the single most important individual in the rise of the Pentecostal movement. His reputation as a small-time faith healer preceded his initiation of Pentecostalism; yet his newfound doctrine did not in any way negate his earlier belief in the divine origins of healing. Like Dowie, Parham believed a cure would come if the seeker would appropriate a radical faith in God's desire and ability to heal. He often denounced doctors and medicines and chided his followers with "Friends, we will never get rid of the devil until we quit this everlasting nursing of our diseases."[7]

Like Parham, all subsequent Pentecostals held a fervent belief in divine healing. All were not as explicit in their denunciation of medical science; yet the idea was implicit that the failure to secure healing was merely a problem with appropriating enough faith to effect a cure. While many frequented doctors and used medicine to allay their sicknesses, others trusted only God in matters of health. The community understood that, while medical practice was not forbidden, it was not the preferable way to secure healing.[8] Parham's emphasis on healing was paralleled by a series of other Pentecostal pioneers, including Maria B. Woodworth-Etter, Aimee Semple McPherson, Charles S. Price, Fred F. Bosworth, and John G. Lake.

Early within Pentecostalism, a dual theology of healing developed. Adherents recognized that healing generally took place in accordance with the "laying on of hands" by the elders of the church as commanded in James 5:14–15. In this communitarian model, the prayer of faith by the individual was bolstered by the prayers of the community—thus effecting a successful cure. Also recognized, though with less regularity, was the "gift of healing" model described in 1 Corinthians 12:9. In this sequence, the healing touch was granted to one specific individual who was endowed with an extraordinary power. Like all healings, however, the faith of the recipient was required to achieve a successful outcome. The distinction was significant, for while healing was a normative part of many Pentecostal services, certain individuals like Parham were understood to have been granted a unique gift of praying for the sick.[9]

The recognition of this individual gift of healing ultimately led to the most explosive period of healing revivalism in American history. Nationally known Pentecostal evangelists such as William Branham, Oral Roberts, Asa A. Allen, and Jack Coe traversed America during the 1950s holding tent revivals that featured their gift of healing to the postwar generation. In the healing revival, extremes were common and ties with Pentecostal denominations strained. Second-generation Pentecostals were not prone to the absolute position of their parents that all believers would be healed.[10] Yet, in more than any other period in the short history of the movement, the theology and practices of the healing revival prompted wide publicity and exposure. The result was fertile ground for the growth of the charismatic revival within mainline churches. In turn, the charismatic movement was infused with a firm interest in and acceptance of the idea of faith healing.[11]

Turning dollar bills into twenties

A firm belief in divine healing is not, however, the only tenet of the faith movement. The belief that faith in God met all human needs led invariably to concern about the material needs of believers. Parham frequently engaged in "faith travel," trusting that God would provide all his necessities. In addition, many early Pentecostal schools were run on the faith principle. They offered their courses without any set tuition, running a shoestring budget which required frequent prayers and fasts to carry the institutions through periods of crisis. Nevertheless, the belief in God's concern for and ability to meet day-to-day needs was tempered by the participants' mistrust of wealth. Few early Pentecostals shared capitalism's faith in the American economic dream. More often than not, they sprang from humble roots and deplored what they perceived to be the affluent environment of the mainline denominations. For most, God's assurance to meet needs simply did not translate into material prosperity.

More overt claims on God's ability to answer financial prayers came with the independent entrepreneurs of the healing revival. The pressing financial needs of the evangelists forced a greater emphasis on the need for giving and, with it, God's promise to bless the cheerful giver. Some, such as A. A. Allen, were blatant in their portrait of a God who specializes in financial miracles. He spellbound his audiences with an account that God once answered his prayer to meet a $410 printing bill by turning the one-dollar bills he had into twenty-dollar bills.

> Of course, some of you do not believe this. Listen, you old skeptic, you don't have to believe it, because it doesn't have to happen to you. But it had to happen to me. I'll tell you why. I decreed a thing. . . . God said "Thou shall decree a thing, and it shall be established unto thee. . . ." I believe I can command God to perform a miracle for you financially. When you do, God can turn dollar bills into twenties.[12]

Allen's explanation of the miracle was a clear pronouncement of the prosperity doctrine that would begin to flourish in the charismatic congregations of the 1960s.[13]

Enter Kenneth Hagin

The individual most responsible for the spread of faith theology among charismatics is evangelist Kenneth Erwin Hagin, Sr. Born in McKinney, Texas, in August 1917, Hagin struggled through a series of debilitating circumstances. Born prematurely with a congenital heart defect, he weighed less than two pounds at birth. After surprising the attending physician by surviving, Hagin endured a painful childhood. At age six, his father deserted the family; shortly thereafter, his mother suffered a nervous breakdown. Worst of all, Hagin failed to outgrow the physical problems that plagued him at birth. By age sixteen, he was bedridden, physically paralyzed, and sometimes unable to maintain consciousness.

While in this state, Hagin began to experience a dramatic inward trauma. On three separate occasions, he believed his spirit slipped from this world, leaving his lifeless body lying on the bed, and descending into the literal pit of hell. Each time, as his spirit trembled at the fires of hell and the loneliness of outer darkness, he was suddenly snatched from the depths of the pit by the voice of God himself and allowed to reenter his body. When he returned the third time, he prayed loudly for God to forgive him of his sins.[14]

During the months that followed, Hagin began a period of intense Bible study and prayer in which he focused on the words of Mark 11:23–24:

> For verily I say unto you, That whosoever shall say unto this mountain, Be thou removed, and be thou cast into the sea; and shall not doubt in his heart, but shall believe that those things which he saith shall come to pass; he shall have whatsoever he saith. Therefore I say unto you, What things soever ye desire, when ye pray, believe that ye receive them, and ye shall have them. (KJV)

Though still near the point of death, he began to pray for God to heal him. Finally, after sixteen months of lying bedfast—praying and studying Mark 11:24 and trying to understand why his healing did not come—Hagin believed he made a remarkable discovery.

In this moment, I saw exactly what that verse in Mark 11:24 meant. Until then I was going to wait till I was actually healed. I was looking at my body and testing my heartbeat to see if I had been healed. But I saw that the verse says that you have to believe when you pray. The *having* comes after the *believing*. I had been reversing it. I was trying to *have* first and then *believe* second. . . . "I see it. I see it," I said with joy. "I see what I've got to do, Lord. I've got to believe that my heart is well while I'm still lying here on this bed, and while my heart is not beating right. I've got to believe that my paralysis is gone while I'm still lying here flat on my back and helpless.[15]

Hagin's discovery culminated in a radical faith that took Mark 11:23–24 literally. It marked his understanding of what he called "the principle of faith": "believe in your heart, say it with your mouth, and 'he shall have whatsoever he saith.' "[16] Exercising his newfound "faith formula," Hagin got up out of his bed, "declared that I was healed and that I was going to walk." For the next few days he walked privately around his room; by the end of the week he was walking downtown.[17]

Hagin's miraculous recovery launched his ministry as a Southern Baptist preacher. His firm belief in divine healing, however, soon placed him in Pentecostal circles, and by 1937 he had received the baptism of the Holy Spirit and joined the Assemblies of God. After pastoring Assemblies churches in Texas for twelve years, Hagin embarked on an independent ministry that would ultimately seal his place as the most prominent of the faith teachers in the coming charismatic revival.[18]

The transformation from Assemblies of God pastor to preeminent faith teacher involved a series of intense religious experiences during which Hagin believed Jesus led him into his true vocation. The first sign in this direction came in 1943 when Hagin suddenly felt that God had placed on him the gift of teaching. Nine years later, after having already stepped out as a "teaching" evangelist within the Pentecostal healing revival, a similar experience convinced him that he was also anointed as a prophet. Significantly, these two "callings" were punctuated by a series of eight visions from 1950 to 1963, during which Hagin believed he conversed with Jesus about this new direction for his ministry and the proper interpretation of certain Scriptures.[19]

A principle theme of these visions was the emphasis on faith without doubt, and the need to confess positively that prayer had been answered—a theme wholly consistent with Hagin's childhood experiences. During this time, Hagin was also heavily influenced by the writings of Essek William Kenyon, an earlier advocate of divine healing whose theology reflected elements of the metaphysical theory of a nineteenth-century philosophical school known as New Thought.[20]

The emphasis on positive confession and the power of individual faith gradually established a separate identity for Hagin's ministry. In 1962, he launched his own evangelistic association. Moving his headquarters to Tulsa, Oklahoma, in 1966, Hagin's ministry finally began a meteoric rise. Riding the crest of the fast-growing charismatic movement, he became, by the early 1980s, one of the nation's best-known evangelists. His daily radio program was carried on 180 stations in the United States and Canada, his monthly *Word of Faith* magazine enjoyed a circulation of 200 thousand, and his $20 million Rhema Bible Training Center enrolled almost two thousand students. Of a total of ten thousand graduates of Rhema, one thousand remained affiliated with Hagin through membership in the Rhema Ministerial Association, an organization that granted them ministerial ordination.[21] More important, Hagin's ministry sponsored other faith teachers. By the late 1980s, Kenneth and Gloria Copeland, Fred Price, Charles Capps, Robert Tilton, and a host of others were citing similar themes and enjoying remarkable success.

The problems with positive confession

Hagin and the other faith teachers have faced increasing criticism for their theology. On one level, their teaching is a restatement of the more extreme positions on divine healing and prosperity present within the Pentecostal tradition. On another level, however, there is a third essential component of the faith movement that is less representative of early Pentecostalism. While Pentecostals were convinced that God had the power and the desire to heal their diseases and meet their needs, they were less sure they had the right to claim healing and financial security in the face of evidence to the contrary. However, charismatic faith teachers, reflecting the metaphysical theories of nineteenth-century transcendentalists and Christian Scientists, as well as Hagin's own personal experience, argued that seekers stopped short of having their prayers answered because they failed to positively confess their triumph in the face of defeat. The result was a profound emphasis on the ability of the believing Christian to effect control over his own situation by the level of his own faith. Crucial was the ability to speak in such a way as to induce, rather than deter, faith. A somewhat sympathetic psychology professor aptly summed up the importance of this aspect when he noted: "What a person says is what a person gets, say all the faith teachers, and this appears to be the keystone of their system."[22]

More than any other single element, positive confession has drawn fire from within Pentecostal and charismatic camps. Critics argue that the language and implications of the faith teachers lends itself to a heretical view of man's importance. God's will becomes dependent on man; the Creator, a kind of "cosmic bellhop" to attend to the needs and desires of his creation.[23] Worse, others charge, man becomes a kind of god himself with the innate ability to control the affairs around him. The result is human pride and a faulty view of both the purpose for and the relationship between God and man.

The movement has also been dubbed gnosticism by some since it tends to focus only on man as a spirit and ignores the traditional balance of body, soul, and spirit within orthodox Christianity. The charge of gnosticism also centers on the dichotomy between "sense knowledge" and "revelation knowledge," a major emphasis in faith teachings. Sense knowledge (i.e., from the senses) should never be trusted or followed, only revelation knowledge (i.e., that which comes through spirit-led interpretation of Scripture). Critics charge that this distinction distorts reality by denying the importance of both a Christian's view of and experience with God.

Still other critics point to the connection with nineteenth-century New Thought metaphysics and denounce the movement as cultic. Acknowledging that some of the faith movement's teachings are biblical, one major charismatic critic charged: "The sad truth is that the cultic, not the biblical, elements of the Faith theology are the very elements that distinguish it the most, cause its amazing growth, and occupy center stage in the Faith movement."[24]

On a different level, critics accuse the faith teachers of distorting Scripture by taking verses out of context to prove their theology.[25] They also point out that there is an explicit rejection of believers who do not get healed or suffer the indignity of poverty, since the only assumption can be that they fail to appropriate faith in God to remedy their situation. More serious is the charge that the rejection of medical science or even the tacit implication that such support is an "inferior" sort of healing leads believers into dangerous situations where they refuse to seek medical help for diseases. The most extreme of the faith teachers, they charge, have so blatantly distorted God's message that they themselves are liable for murder.[26]

Such fears seemed realized in 1984 when a storm of publicity surrounded the death of a fifteen-year-old girl whose parents had refused medical assistance on counsel from faith teacher Hobart Freeman. The girl subsequently died of kidney failure, and physicians agreed the death could have been prevented with proper medical treatment. Freeman's indictment on a charge of "aiding and inducing reckless homicide" fueled the fire of national attention, as critics charged that some ninety deaths within Freeman's small circle of Faith Assembly churches ultimately had their roots in his teachings. When Freeman died unexpectedly in December 1984, his part in what might have been a national trial drama was abruptly ended; nevertheless, the furor over the dangers inherent in faith theology remained high within Pentecostal and charismatic circles.[27]

Faith teachers on the defensive

Faith teachers have answered their critics in a variety of ways. All major leaders of the movement denounce the position of extremists like Freeman and his Faith Assembly. They teach that medical science in and of itself is not evil and urge followers to seek medical advice if they have any doubt as to their faith. Hagin points out that there are no "iron clad rules" in dealing with individuals. While "God's best is that we be healed by divine power," individual ability to believe will mean that "not everyone will attain to the best."[28]

Leaders like Hagin also argue that their teachings are simply God's Word and cite a number of scriptural "proof texts" on their behalf. They qualify the criticism of those who see only the "name it–claim it" philosophy by pointing out that all desires are to be based on Scripture alone.

> We've got a right to claim anything the Bible says is ours. But if you go off claiming something else, that's a different thing. We've got a right to claim salvation; it belongs to us. We've got a right to claim healing, to claim the baptism in the Holy Ghost, to claim that our needs will be met.

> Now when you get beyond anything the Bible says, then you'd better have a revelation from God before you can have faith for it. Faith begins where the will of God is known. The Bible is the will of God.[29]

Hagin also takes issue with the charge that faith theology is essentially New Thought metaphysics. Admitting that some movements, like positive thinking, work because they apply biblical principles, he nonetheless dismisses the parallel argument that he does not teach positive thinking, only that the Bible is positively true. The comparison is faulty, he maintains, since "just because they have discovered some principles that sound a whole lot like what we're saying, it doesn't mean it *is* the same."[30]

Health and wealth today

The faith movement grew extensively in the 1970s because of the growth rate of the charismatic movement. Attracted by its biblical literalism as well as its promise of the supernatural in the church's everyday life, many young, educated, affluent charismatics climbed on the bandwagon. With scientific studies validating the beneficial effects of positive meditation and prayer, and President Jimmy Carter's sister, Ruth Stapleton, a visible exponent of divine healing, the faith movement picked up many who in earlier years would merely have scoffed at its claims.[31]

In addition, the faith movement benefited from the national obsession with health, as the nation's median age climbed higher with the ending of the post–World War II baby boom. Television exposure also played a role in the new success. Multimedia ministries flooded the airways with religious talk shows and devotionals.

And taking prime advantage of these opportunities were the new charismatic ministers; once in the living room, they benefited from the power of television to get their message across.

Finally, the faith message enjoyed the effects of prosperity among the old-line Pentecostals. Joining the numbers of charismatics who embraced the faith message was a significant number of third- and fourth-generation Pentecostals whose economic status had risen considerably as a result of educational gains during the postwar era. The newer churches offered them the emotional worship style of their parent denominations in a socio-economic climate that better fit their new situation.

By 1979, the faith movement was large enough to form a loose association, the International Convention of Faith Churches and Ministers, to coordinate activities and provide a forum for regional and national conferences. By the mid-1980s, the association affiliated over seven hundred faith ministers.[32]

However, controversy over the faith movement continues. Critics outside of the charismatic movement often accuse the faith teachers of outright charlatanry. Specifically, they point out that faith theology gives all the credit for miraculous cures to the faith teacher and places all blame for failure on the "unbelieving" seeker. More important to the future of the faith movement is the criticism from within the charismatic movement. Faith theology caused a minor schism at Oral Roberts University in the early 1980s, as the pre-eminent figure of the Pentecostal healing revival developed closer ties to the major faith evangelists. Though not an explicit proponent of faith theology himself, Oral Roberts nevertheless has bordered on many of its theological precepts throughout his ministry. Yet even Roberts's considerable prestige has not been enough to protect the faith movement from criticism.[33] While some believe that the faith teachers have moderated their more extreme positions in the wake of the Hobart Freeman debacle, others express their doubts. The result is a continuing debate over the merits and dangers of the movement.[34]

That the faith movement will survive seems certain. Yet the power and credibility of the movement has always been tied to the fortunes of the larger charismatic movement. As tensions continue to break out, the possibility of a break from other Pentecostals and charismatics becomes increasingly likely. The result of such a break would render the faith movement a much smaller component outside its natural spawning ground. Such a break would also continue a long-standing tradition in American religious history by further splinter- ing the increasingly heterogeneous charismatic revival.

Notes

1. Though D. R. McConnell argues in *A Different Gospel: A Histori- cal and Biblical Analysis of the Modern Faith Movement* (Peabody, Mass.: Hendrickson, 1988) that the movement moved toward de- nominational status with the establishment of the International Convention of Faith Churches and Ministers in 1979 (see pp. 85–7), there is no uniform organizational structure and thus no incorporated name.

2. The lively debate is clearly seen in the different tactics chosen by two researchers, both of whom describe themselves as charismatic. Bruce Barron's *The Health and Wealth Gospel* (Downers Grove, Ill.: InterVarsity Press, 1987) is a sympathetic appeal for balance and understanding. He argues that many aspects of the faith movement are valuable, though extremes are potentially dangerous. McCon- nell, on the other hand, presents an outright attack on both the historical origins and theological positions of the faith movement, describing it as "cultic" and "heretical." See McConnell, pp. xiii–xviii.

3. Donald Dayton, "The Rise of the Evangelical Healing Move- ment in Nineteenth Century America," *Pneuma* 4 (Spring 1982), p. 6. For a good, broad survey of healing movements in America, see Paul Chappell's "Healing Movements" in Stanley M. Burgess and Gary B. McGee, eds., *Dictionary of Pentecostal and Charismatic Movements* (Grand Rapids, Mich.: Zondervan Publishing House, 1988), pp. 353–74.

4. On Dowie, see Burgess and McGee, pp. 366–7 and Grant Wacker, "Marching to Zion: Religion in a Modern Utopian Commu- nity" *Church History* 54 (December 1985), pp. 496–511.

5. Dayton, p. 18.

6. Morton T. Kelsey's *Psychology, Medicine and Christian Healing*

(San Francisco: Harper & Row, 1988) erroneously claims that the healing ministry of the Pentecostal revival was "only incidental to their emphasis on tongue speaking and other gifts of the Spirit" (p. 2). He argues that healing "came as a surprise to many leaders of the movement, since few of them knew about the long and continuous ministry of healing of the early church" (p. 192). For support of my position, see Burgess and McGee, p. 353.

7. James R. Goff, Jr., *Fields White Unto Harvest: Charles F. Parham and the Missionary Origins of Pentecostalism* (Fayetteville: University of Arkansas Press, 1988), p. 43.

8. Parham is typical of the Pentecostals who sought this "higher level" of healing. There is no evidence that, after totally accepting divine healing in 1897, he ever used medicine or sought the advice of a physician again. He died in 1929 at the age of 55; Goff, pp. 39 and 159. The issue was explosive enough to precipitate a split in the Pentecostal Holiness Church in the 1920s. See Vinson Synan, *The Old-Time Power* (Franklin Springs, Ga.: Advocate Press, 1973), pp. 165–71.

9. Parham was widely believed to have the gift of healing though he himself never personally claimed it. See Sarah E. Parham, *Life of Charles F. Parham* (Joplin, Mo.: Tri-State Printing Co., 1930), p. 33.

10. Walter J. Hollenweger, *The Pentecostals* (Minneapolis, Minn.: Augsburg Publishing House, 1972), p. 357.

11. David Edwin Harrell, Jr., *All Things Are Possible: The Healing and Charismatic Revivals in Modern America* (Bloomington: Indiana University Press, 1975), pp. 135–49.

12. Ibid., p. 75.

13. Ibid., pp. 104–6 and 229.

14. Hagin's dramatic experience is recounted in Kenneth E. Hagin, *I Believe in Visions* (Old Tappan, N.J.: Fleming H. Revell Company, 1972), pp. 9–18. See also McConnell, pp. 58–60.

15. Ibid., pp. 27–28. Also McConnell, p. 59.

16. Ibid., p. 26.

17. Ibid., pp. 29–30.

18. Ibid., pp. 30–39. Also McConnell, pp. 60–61 and Barron, pp. 47–49.

19. Hagin's account of these visions forms the major content of his widely distributed *I Believe in Visions*.

20. On Hagin's connection to Kenyon and New Thought, see McConnell, pp. 3–76.

21. Burgess and McGee, pp. 373–4, McConnell, p. 78, and Bob Anthony, "America's Faith Movement: Finding the Balance" *Bridgebuilder* (May–June 1989), p. 17.

22. Donald L. Clark, "An Implicit Theory of Personality, Illness, and Cure Found in the Writings of Neo-Pentecostal Faith Teachers," *Journal of Psychology and Theology* 12 (Fall 1984), p. 282.

23. William W. Menzies, "Will Charismatics Go Cultic?" *Christianity Today* 33 (March 3, 1989), p. 59.

24. McConnell, p. 51.

25. Verses often accused of being interpreted out of context are Proverbs 6:2, Romans 10:8, Romans 4:17, and 3 John 2. Burgess and McGee, pp. 719–20.

26. Barron, pp. 77–87.

27. Ibid., pp. 14–34. See also Randy Frame, "Indiana Grand Jury Indicts a Faith-Healing Preacher," *Christianity Today* (Nov. 23, 1984), pp. 38–39 and Chris Lutes, "Leader's Death Gives Rise to Speculation About the Future of His Faith-Healing Sect," *Christianity Today* (Jan. 18, 1985), p. 48. Similar charges were sometimes leveled at early Pentecostal preachers. See Goff, pp. 93–94 and 142–43.

28. Anthony, p. 18.

29. Ibid.

30. Ibid.

31. For examples of favorable press toward healing advocates, see Kenneth L. Woodward, "The Cures Doctors Can't Explain," *McCall's* 102 (April 1975), pp. 87, 126–8; Jessamyn West, "Jimmy Carter's Sister: 'How Faith Can Heal,' " *McCall's* 104 (April 1977), pp. 32, 34–42; "Science Takes New Look at Faith Healing," *U. S. News & World Report* 86 (Feb. 12, 1979), pp. 68–69; Kenneth L. Woodward, "The New Healers," *Newsweek* 92 (July 17, 1978), pp. 60–61; and "In a New Book, a Doctor Links Prayer and Physical Healing," *Christianity Today* 28 (May 18, 1984), pp. 96–100.

32. McConnell, pp. 85–87.

33. On the controversy at ORU, see David E. Harrell, Jr., *Oral Roberts: An American Life* (San Francisco: Harper & Row, 1985), pp. 422–7. Roberts's own philosophy on health and prosperity is aptly

described in his *Three Most Important Steps to Your Better Health and Miracle Living* (Tulsa: Oral Roberts Evangelistic Association, Inc., 1976).

34. For a favorable assessment, see Barron's "Faith Healers: Moving Toward the Mainstream," *Christianity Today*, 31 (July 10, 1987), p. 52. For evidence of continuing controversy, see McConnell, pp. 184–90 and "Fuller Seminary Releases Study on the Miraculous," *Christianity Today* 31 (Feb. 6, 1987), pp. 44–45.

Chapter 6

SALVATION SHOCK TROOPS

L. Grant McClung, Jr.

"God has truly raised up this 'Third Force' in the 20th century to 'hasten the coming' of His day through accelerating the missionary obedience of His Church."
—Arthur F. Glasser, 1985

Pentecostals have been probed, promoted, dismissed, and discussed from every possible category—theological, sociological, historical, phenomenological, psychological. And yet Pentecostalism cannot be properly or accurately described without understanding its *own self-identity* as a missionary movement raised up by God to evangelize the world in the last days. Thus, Assemblies of God missions historian Gary B. McGee rightly asserts that "the history of Pentecostalism cannot be properly understood apart from its missionary vision."

That missionary vision, however, is a "mixed bag," forged out of a number of converging streams. McGee points out that the call to overseas evangelism comes out of a "close and abiding association" between the baptism of the Holy Spirit (confirmed by speaking in tongues) as the supernatural provision of power for witnessing, a fervent belief in the premillennial return of Christ, and a desire to be as obedient as possible to Christ's command to make disciples in the uttermost parts of the world.

"Understood as the theology of 'last things,'" said Prudencio Damboriena, "eschatology belongs to the essence of Pentecostalism." And an often critical Frederick Bruner stated that "Pentecostalism and mission are almost synonymous." Pioneer Pentecostal zealots and today's Pentecostal missiologists would remove the qualifying "almost" from Bruner's observation and assert that, from the beginning, the mission of the Pentecostal movement *was* mission.

A fundamental question must be raised, however, given the insights of Damboriena and Bruner: If Pentecostals are typified by an "ethos of growth," it is important to ask, "What kind of growth?" Missiologist David Hesselgrave asks, with some justification, whether today's charismatics are more interested in making converts to a particular spiritual experience from an already professing segment of the Christian church than they are in making new converts to Christ from the secular/pagan world.

The same criticism was leveled at early Pentecostals. John Thomas Nichol (*Pentecostalism*, Harper & Row, 1966) claimed that early Pentecostals saw themselves as a revitalization movement within the church. They made their early thrusts, therefore, toward nominal Christians and lethargic believers rather than toward the unconverted. But Hesselgrave notes that the early Pentecostal revivals were marked with a mission vision "from the very first."

Thus, while Pentecostals focused their early efforts on professing Christians, their goal was to mobilize these revitalized saints with new anointing toward reaching the lost. This is the sense of the opening lines of the first issue of *The Apostolic Faith*, the newsletter from the Azusa Street Mission (September 1906):

Pentecost has surely come and with it the Bible evidences are following, many being converted and sanctified and filled with the Holy Ghost, speaking in tongues as they did on the day of Pentecost . . . the real revival is only started, as God has been working with His children mostly, getting them through to Pentecost, and laying the foundation for a mighty wave of salvation among the unconverted.

A year later, the publication stressed that "the heathen must first receive the gospel" (as a prerequisite to the Lord's return); and "the only way the nations can be reached is by getting the missionaries baptized with the Holy Ghost."

If, then, early Pentecostals felt their preaching to the unreached would hasten the coming of the Lord, then it stands to reason that they would not be satisfied with promoting a new spiritual experience among the saints only. The sooner they could reach the world of unbelieving humanity, the sooner the King would return. Pentecostalism cannot be dismissed, therefore, as a potpourri of luxurious spiritual experiences for the elect. William J. Seymour, the black leader of the Azusa Street Mission, would constantly urge his people, "Now, do not go from this meeting and talk about tongues, but try to get people saved." Modern Pentecostals, particularly those in North America, would do well to remind themselves that the spiritual enablement inherent in the Pentecostal experience is more than peace, power, and prosperity, more than a prayer language or a higher dimension of faith, but an endowment of divine power to reach a lost world.

End-times expectancy
Eschatological urgency was nothing new to Pentecostalism. Premillennial teaching and dispensationalism gave rise to a number of movements in the nineteenth century, urging world evangelization in light of the imminent return of Christ. Among these were the Student Volunteer Movement for Foreign Missions and the Dwight L. Moody revival campaigns. Moody confided that he "felt like working three times as hard ever since I came to understand that my Lord was coming back again." When premillennialism impacted the holiness movement with such strong advocates as Moody and A. B. Simpson, the stage was set for a dynamic missionary thrust.

Eschatology was the life blood of Simpson's missionary theology. He held that Christians were living in the "last days" of Joel 2:28–32 and that the evangelization of the lost world could only be accomplished by a mighty outpouring of the Holy Spirit.

As the end of the century approached, the holiness and "higher life" advocates had produced missions and prayer movements that earnestly sought divine enablement (using language such as "the baptism of the Holy Ghost") and expected Christ's appearing.

Salvation shock troops

While the signs and wonders of Azusa Street have already been discussed in earlier chapters, it is important to emphasize the critical missions dimension of this three-year revival. McGee says at least three things happened that influenced early conceptions of Pentecostal theology and practice.

The first had to do with a missionary understanding of the practice of speaking in tongues. Believers experienced the power of God in the prayer meetings and often spoke in tongues that were recognizable foreign languages. Many foreign immigrants were present in Los Angeles, and a number were attracted to the prayer meetings. In numerous cases, they were converted through the powerful and convicting messages conveyed supernaturally to them in their own languages. Azusa Street recipients assumed that God was giving them the ability to preach in other lands and often discerned a call to a particular country based upon the language they had spoken. *The Apostolic Faith* reported, "The gift of languages is given with the commission."

The practice of missionary tongues was undergirded by such accounts as that of A. G. Ward, a pioneer minister among the Indians in Canada. One day while preaching through an interpreter, Ward suddenly began speaking in other tongues. His surprised interpreter exclaimed, "Why, you are now speaking to us in our own language!" (Assemblies of God historian Stanley Frodsham devoted an entire chapter to such incidents in his midcentury reflection, *With Signs Following* [Gospel Publishing House, 1946].)*

---

*Ralph Harris, another Assemblies of God researcher, devoted an entire book to the subject as recently as 1973. In his *Spoken by the Spirit* (Gospel Publishing House), Harris argues that *xenolalia*, or *xenoglossolalia*, is characteristic of *contemporary* Pentecostalism as well as that

Charles Parham and others influenced by him at Azusa Street taught that missionaries would no longer need to study foreign languages in order to preach on the mission field. However, after many fiascos and disappointments, most Pentecostal leaders departed from this belief. Missionary tongues, or *xenolalia*, was taken as the exception rather than the rule.

A second conviction seized the Azusa Street recipients: They believed the "signs and wonders" of apostolic times were being restored in a "latter rain" of end-time power just prior to the personal, visible, literal return of Christ and the inauguration of his reign. Theirs was now a "mission on the verge"; something was about to happen! An apocalyptic excitement gripped them:

> There is no man at the head of this movement. God Himself is speaking in the earth. We are on the verge of the greatest miracle the world has ever seen, when the sons of God shall be manifested, the saints shall come singing from the dust (Isa. 26:19) and the full overcomers shall be caught up to meet the Lord in the air. The political world realizes that some great crisis is at hand, the scientific world, the religious world all feel it. The coming of the Lord draweth nigh, it is near, even at the doors. (In the first issue of *The Apostolic Faith*, September 1906)

This intense premillennialism led to the third and consequential development: a prompt mobilization of new missionaries for the field. Due to the urgency of the hour, scores of new recruits took off to the far-flung corners of the earth, expecting Jesus to come at any moment and knowing that they had the language to preach the gospel through the gift of tongues.

These early evangelists—many ill-trained and ill-financed—were supernaturally recruited in a variety of ways through dreams and visions, prophecy, tongues and interpretations, and inner impressions. Some claimed to hear the audible voice of God or have certain portions of Scripture customized with specific revelations during their Bible reading.

reported in the days of Azusa Street. He collected case studies from more than sixty languages, his informants coming from a wide spectrum, his results documented and verified.

Robert Cook was an Azusa Street participant who went to India as an independent missionary and later joined the Church of God. He tells the story of how God confirmed his leading to India and convinced his wife that they should go. In order for his wife to be assured of the Lord's leading, he says:

> He gave her the name of a town in South India, of which she was quite ignorant at the time. She and a friend, Esther Lampert, were sitting on the floor while Esther was tuning Wife's guitar; suddenly Wife spoke out, "Bangalore."
>
> Sister Esther looked up and said, "Did you say 'Tune lower?' "
>
> "No," said Wife, "I heard a voice saying 'Bangalore' and I repeated it."
>
> When I came home, they told me of this, and I said, "Why, that is the town where the missionary with whom we are going has lived."

A theology on the move

Pentecostal mission theology has tended to be a "theology on the move," often acting now and theologizing later. It has been more experiential than cognitive, more activist than reflective, more actualized than analyzed. Only recently have Pentecostal missiologists begun to solidify a more formalized Pentecostal missions theology.

This is not to suggest that the pioneer Pentecostals were without theological assumptions. Indeed, at least five "answers" could have been given to the question, "What do Pentecostals believe about mission?"

1. Pentecostal missiology is *obedient*. Pentecostals have been marked by their exactness in following a literal interpretation of Scripture, with the Book of Acts serving as their model for apostolic ministry. For them, the issue of biblical authority is nonnegotiable and is the beginning point for missions theology and strategy. They have understood world evangelization as one of the primary steps of obedience in Christian discipleship. This high regard for Scripture caused Pentecostals to conclude that mankind is lost and under the judgment of eternal punishment unless reached with the good news of the gospel. The doctrinal confessions of all major Pentecostal

organizations reflect their belief in "eternal life for the righteous, and eternal punishment for the wicked" with no liberation or annihilation (in terms of "second chance" salvation). Imagine the sense of awe and dread imposed upon these early pioneers when they believed they had been raised up to bear this sobering message to the nations before it was eternally too late.

2. Pentecostal missiology is *expectant*. Spirit-energized witnesses fanned out across the nation and around the world, enduring persecution and adverse conditions because they expected the "any moment" return of Jesus. And not only did they expect his imminent return, but they expected God to reveal himself to them in unusual ways. That is why Loren Cunningham could testify of a life-changing vision at age thirteen in which he saw the bold letters conveying the commission: GO YE INTO ALL THE WORLD AND PREACH THE GOSPEL TO EVERY CREATURE. The young Pentecostal went on to preach the gospel and eventually started today's largest nondenominational faith mission, Youth With A Mission. Such an occurrence was not foreign to early Pentecostals.

3. Pentecostal missiology is *activist*. Favorite verses of Pentecostal missionaries were Mark 16:15–18 (emphasizing signs and wonders), Acts 1:8 (promising the power available to go to the ends of the earth), and Matthew 24:14, "This gospel of the kingdom shall be preached in all the world for a witness unto all nations; and then shall the end come." Thus A. B. Simpson's cry, "Bring Back the King" gained popular acceptance throughout the ranks of Pentecostal missionaries—and they got on with the job.

Today, more than eighty years after Azusa Street, that inherent Pentecostal activism is vibrant in missionary circles. G. Edward Nelson's challenge (in *Mountain Movers*, the foreign missions magazine of the Assemblies of God, August 1988) bears amazing resemblance to historic claims from the early years:

> The Church is on the verge of the greatest moment in history—the witness of the gospel to all nations and the second coming of Jesus Christ. . . . The imminence of His coming is connected to the completion of the Church's mission to bear testimony of Christ's kingdom to every nation.

Mainline Pentecostals are careful to avoid "calendarizing," however (today, more than in the movement's past). For them, premillennialism is a reason to *proclaim*, not to *predict*. Eschatology and evangelization work together. Pentecostals preach because they believe the end is coming; they believe the end is coming because they preach.

4. Pentecostal missiology is *anointed*. David du Plessis called it "truth on fire." J. Roswell Flower stressed "apostolic ministry in apostolic power." Pentecostal missionaries insisted that God was to be experienced personally through the Holy Spirit. For them, the Holy Spirit is personally active, living in and directing his servants in world evangelization.

The passion for souls, said British Pentecostal leader Donald Gee, and the desire for spiritual gifts were mutually inclusive, not exclusive. Many followed the lead of J. Roswell Flower, a Midwestern Pentecostal editor/publisher, in making the connection between passion and power more than an observation, but a prescription:

> The baptism of the Holy Ghost does not consist in simply speaking in tongues. No. It has a much more grand and deeper meaning than that. It fills our souls with the love of God for lost humanity, and makes us much more willing to leave home, friends, and all to work in His vineyard, even if it be far away among the heathen. . . .
>
> "Go ye into all the world and preach the gospel to every creature." This command of Jesus can only be properly fulfilled when we have obeyed that other command, "Tarry ye in the City of Jerusalem til ye be endued with power from on high." When we have tarried and received that power, then, and then only are we fit to carry the gospel. When the Holy Spirit comes into our hearts, the missionary spirit comes in with it; they are inseparable, as the missionary spirit is but one of the fruits of the Holy Spirit. Carrying the gospel to hungry souls in this and other lands is but a natural result of receiving the baptism of the Holy Ghost.

5. Pentecostal missiology is *optimistic*. Though formed through the rhetoric of impending doom, Pentecostals have not overlooked the "latter rain" promises of worldwide revival. They have felt very self-assured (some would say "triumphal" and arrogant) in their

place in God's final salvation history. Pentecostals are task oriented and believe the job of world evangelization can be done. They freely identify with the *countdown* and *closure* language of contemporary evangelical missiology (toward the year 2000), and they have aggressive plans to move through the decade of the nineties with intentional harvesting.

In an introspection that was both self-critical yet self-affirming, Vinson Synan stated in preparation for the 1987 General Congress on the Holy Spirit and World Evangelization in New Orleans:

> We've been in the upper room with our spiritual gifts. But we are supposed to go to the streets with our tongues and healings and prophecies. We believe the Pentecostals and charismatics have been raised up by God as the shock troops for the greatest final assault on the enemy.

The clearly stated primary goal of the convocation was to motivate Pentecostals and charismatics to bring the "majority of the human race to Jesus Christ by the end of the century."

The last age of missions?
Where such missionary zeal will take the movement, only God knows. But could upwardly mobile, middle-class Pentecostals and charismatics be flexing their muscles too much, expecting too great a franchise in getting the kingdom in place—now? Historian William Menzies cautions that some younger Pentecostals are expressing a new fascination with an "emerging order," an overconfident assurance that this present order can be transformed and made ready for the coming of its King.

The basic problem, missiologically, with this revived postmillennialism (called variously "Kingdom Now," "Dominion Theology," or "Reconstructionism") is its inward preoccupation with the survival of itself and the disenfranchisement of the nations (counting more than three billion yet unreached). Proponents charge that missions and evangelism are too narrow for the transformation of social structures. But what is overlooked, says Menzies, "is that Pentecostals have quietly gone about social renewal in unobtrusive ways, working with the poor of this world in unheralded corners."

From the "unheralded corners" now comes a new Pentecostal and charismatic surge in missions from the Third World, the so-called emerging missions from non-Western sources. Pentecostal theologian Russell Spittler has predicted that the first "truly indigenous Pentecostal theology will emerge from the Third World, specifically Latin America."

Third World Pentecostals and charismatics are taking the lead in church growth, theologizing, and effectively struggling with issues of social justice. Now, world evangelization is high on their agenda. With efforts such as the COMIBAM movement (the Ibero-American Missionary Congress), traditional "mission fields" are signaling their move to a "missionary force." Pentecostals and charismatics are deeply involved in this transdenominational advance (as they are in the Lausanne movement) to bring about what missiologist Lawrence Keyes has called *The Last Age of Missions* (William Carey Library, 1983).

As a case in point, consider Calvary Charismatic Center in Southeast Asia's city-state of Singapore. Calvary is Singapore's largest church, having grown from a handful of believers in 1977 to over five thousand ten years later. In their aggressive foreign missions program, members give some $1.2 million per year to world evangelization. During the last half of the eighties, the church sent over two hundred people on short-term planting teams to more than a dozen countries. As a result, about one-third of these short-termers chose full-time missionary service.

A review of the historical/theological dynamics in the spread of early Pentecostalism around the world reveals a clear-cut, if not yet systematic, theology of missions. But it is important for Pentecostals not to rest upon the heritage and experiences of another generation. Instead, they must missionize in the power of the Holy Spirit today and tomorrow until the end comes.

AMERICA'S PENTECOSTALS: WHERE THEY ARE GOING

Chapter 7

THE GREAT TRANSMISSION

Quentin J. Schultze

Of all the major groups within the mosaic of American evangelicalism, Pentecostals have most easily and effectively adapted their message to the broadcast media. Radio and television were ripe for Pentecostalism's dramatic and highly emotional expression of the Christian faith. As a result, broadcasting and Pentecostalism served each other well, although neither has remained unaffected by the sometimes turbulent partnership.

Crystal-set soul winning
Aimee Semple McPherson established one of the first popular religious radio stations in 1924. "An almost unbelievable miracle has happened to the modern preacher," she told her followers at Angelus Temple. "Imagine being seated comfortably in your own home and

hearing a whole church service being rendered four thousand miles away! Imagine the feeling of being able to participate in the whole service . . . winning souls by speaking through the air. . . . We fully expect to reach with the preached word the prairie wife and her little family; the mountaineer amid the rugged crag and timbers of his alpine abode; the desert dweller amidst the sand dunes, cactus and sage brush; the indian [sic] chief with his followers in Mojave reservations; the blue jacket who sails in Uncle Sam's warships; the cripple in the wheelchair; the businessman as he sits at his luncheon."

McPherson's dream was shared by thousands of Pentecostal preachers who took to the radio during the twenty-five years before television. But the dream frequently led to controversy as Pentecostalism clashed with American culture and even with itself. "A world war is the only thing that could have reduced Aimee Semple McPherson to an inside page position," wrote a Los Angeles reporter in 1942. Like most Pentecostal broadcasters who followed in her footsteps, McPherson was contentious and colorful. A magazine wrote that in "show-devouring" Los Angeles, "no entertainment compares in popularity with that of Angelus Temple; the audience, whether devout or otherwise, concede it the best for the money (or no money) in town."

Faced with the expense of running a station and Federal Communications Commission policies that discriminated against religious stations, Pentecostals did remarkably well. McPherson's KFSG (Kall Four Square Gospel) radio and the Pillar of Fire, which operated stations in Denver and New Jersey, were three of only a handful of noncommercial AM radio stations to survive until the 1960s.

The success of syndicated Pentecostal broadcasts was even more amazing. A study conducted in 1937 of 425 radio stations found that holiness and Pentecostal broadcasters were the fifth largest in the nation, behind the Baptist, Gospel, Roman Catholic, and Methodist programs. Two-thirds of all of the holiness and Pentecostal broadcasts were reported as "commercial" air time paid for by the religious sponsor. By contrast, the Roman Catholics and Methodists received most of their air time free of charge. Both in their radio stations and syndicated programs, Pentecostals proved already in the 1930s that they could finance influential broadcast operations through contributions.

From tent meeting to television screen

Unlike the dull programming created by most religious groups, Pentecostal broadcasts took advantage of the lessons learned by secular programmers. McPherson's KFSG, for example, aired its own dramatic series such as "Jim Trask Lone Evangelist" and "Half-way House." It also broadcast a popular amateur talent show. Thompson Eade, a former vaudeville performer, created many of KFSG's prime-time programs.

Pentecostals were at the forefront of early television evangelism as well. Rex Humbard pioneered the transition from tent revival to television screen in 1953, when he aired his first program. Humbard's "Cathedral of Tomorrow" television program, eventually aired on over six hundred stations, was named after his Akron church—probably the first one built as a television studio. Sometimes called the "Lawrence Welk of religious broadcasting," Humbard successfully combined the television variety show and the old-fashioned gospel revival. His family sang and Humbard preached.

Working out of the "ghetto"

Humbard's only significant television competition from Protestants during the 1950s, Oral Roberts, similarly fashioned middle-class programming out of Pentecostal revivalism. Roberts began in television in 1954 with the unsuccessful "Your Faith Is Power" show, a thirty-minute healing program that lacked the excitement of his tent services. He returned to the tube in 1955 with filmed versions of his actual tent crusades, claiming that the Holy Spirit was healing viewers as well as those who attended the crusades. Roberts financed the enormous costs of television production and air time by promising contributors that they could have their money back if the Lord had not blessed them financially within a year. Determined to reach mainstream America, not just the Sunday-morning "religious ghetto," he hired a talented musical writer and director, who had composed scores for prime-time television specials, and a Hollywood producer from the golden years of variety shows.

Roberts's first "Contact" special was broadcast in 1969, shortly after he left the Pentecostal Holiness church to become a Methodist minister. It featured the fashionably dressed World Action Singers in a typically glamorous Hollywood-style stage setting. Roberts's later prime-time specials included Christian celebrities from the emerging evangelical entertainment industry—Pat Boone, Dale Evans, and Anita Bryant. Many evangelicals condemned the worldly, show-business culture depicted on the show, and Pentecostals were the harshest critics. But the ratings increased, and the ministry's mail response soared. Roberts was not about to fight success. By 1972, the specials were aired on more than four hundred stations.

Compared with the tent revivals, Roberts's own television role was greatly diminished; he was allowed only eleven minutes for a sermon. Nevertheless, the evening time slot and creative programming gained national publicity for the evangelist, who soon found himself on the talk-show circuit. Eventually tiring of the format, Roberts discontinued the prime-time specials in 1979 and began experimenting with various daily and weekly programs, none of which were as successful.

Widely criticized for some of his fund-raising methods, and suffering serious audience declines, Roberts eventually dropped the syndicated broadcasts in 1988. His son, Richard, played an increasingly important role in the TV ministry, which was limited largely to the cable networks. Roberts reclaimed some of his old-style Pentecostalism as he and Richard searched for an effective program strategy and fund-raising appeal. However, even healing programs and "seed faith" preaching, which encouraged viewers to donate to the ministry knowing that God would multiply their gifts, did little for his sagging ratings. Roberts was lost in the confusing shuffle of religious broadcasters and evangelical audiences. More than anything else, he needed younger viewers, but other televangelists, especially Oral Roberts University graduate Kenneth Copeland, had stepped in to claim that market. In 1988, the Methodist Church took away Roberts's ministerial credentials; he was a sinking religious broadcaster caught in the cultural shifts he helped bring about.

Signs, wonders, and self-indulgence

During the 1980s, the remarkable popularity of Pentecostal broadcasts continued under new names. So did the progressive shift from a hard-core, second-birth message to a new-styled Pentecostalism that combined New Testament "signs and wonders" with the self-indulgence of the Hollywood culture. The charismatic movement, in particular, provided new nondenominational markets for Pentecostal programming. Over half of the ten highest-rated weekly religious television programs in the late 1980s were Pentecostal. They included Oral Roberts, Pat Robertson, Jimmy Swaggart, Jim Bakker, Kenneth Copeland, and Rex Humbard. Moreover, the three largest cable television religious networks—CBN, PTL, and TBN—were founded by Pentecostals and supported extensively by charismatics.

On most of the programs, denominational loyalties were played down in order to maximize audiences and cultivate contributors. The Assemblies of God (AOG) had the largest number of successful national religious broadcasters, but none of them was sponsored by the denomination. On the contrary, the AOG benefited both from the donations received from member televangelists and from audience response. "The 700 Club," in particular, led many non-Pentecostals to the AOG through local church follow-up of viewer telephone calls to the program. (The AOG's own official program, "Revivaltime," was virtually unknown compared to some of the parachurch broadcasts sponsored by the church's independent-minded ministers, including Swaggart and Bakker.)

Among the major Pentecostals on television, however, only Jimmy Swaggart represented the traditional style and substance of the faith. The highest-rated weekly televangelist, he regularly fired salvos at charismatics who accommodated their lifestyles to the values of contemporary middle-class America. A harsh critic of rock music, he called it "spiritual fornication" and condemned its producers and distributors. Swaggart leveled vicious charges against the works-righteousness of the Roman Catholic Church, the predestination of Calvinism, and dozens of other theological doctrines he despised. Swaggart called repeatedly for "Holy Ghost revival" and blasted churches and pastors who did not practice speaking in tongues. Most controversial of all, Swaggart criticized the weak faith of Christians who rely upon psychological counseling or other "humanistic" methods of healing. Swaggart himself claimed in 1988 to be healed from a long-time obsession with pornography that became public when photographs were taken of the evangelist leaving a hotel room with a known prostitute.

Defrocked in 1988 by the AOG for refusing to submit to its discipline, Swaggart soon saw his program dropped by some of the Pentecostal cable networks and even a few commercial television stations. His audience of over two million viewers declined significantly, contributions plunged from their previous high of nearly $500,000 per day, and his program dropped from first place in the weekly ratings. Robert Schuller of the "Hour of Power" program from the Crystal Cathedral, an occasional target of Swaggart's criticisms, moved into the number-one spot.

The Christian Broadcasting Network
Other major styles of broadcast Pentecostalism also reflected important movements in the faith. Television preachers such as Jim Bakker and Pat Robertson appealed to a wide variety of evangelical and charismatic viewers. Highly tolerant of the many doctrinal differences within evangelicalism, they shied away from most theological disputes and emphasized a unifying message of personal salvation and an upbeat promise of personal success, although with very different styles. "Remember, we are a mass media [sic]," said Robertson. "I would rather define those areas where there is unity, than try to pick apart the areas of disagreement."

Robertson's Christian Broadcasting Network (CBN) began in 1961 on a radio and television station the evangelist acquired in Virginia. Using "telethons" to raise money for expansion, Robertson added additional stations in the 1960s and early 1970s, when he began syndicating the program extensively to nonreligious stations across the country. The format of the network's flagship program, "The 700 Club," was based largely on a Gallup study of the Christian marketplace that showed that both Christians and non-Christians preferred a magazine format to typical Sunday-morning preaching. Moreover, "The 700 Club" made miracles the central focus of the program because audience research showed that such a format would produce the largest ratings. "When we started talking about the miracle power of God," said Robertson, "our male audience increased by 67 percent, our female audience went up by 37 percent, and total households watching us increased by 50 percent."

In 1977, Robertson parlayed his various radio and television stations into one of the largest cable TV networks in the country, CBN Cable. Five years later, he positioned it in the secular cable industry as a "family" channel and turned most of its broadcast time over to commercial network reruns. Soon CBN Cable programming resembled typical network fare; the daily schedule included situation comedies from the 1950s and 1960s, action shows, and even old westerns. The ratings increased dramatically, and a growing number of local cable systems added CBN Cable to their basic service. By the end of 1985, CBN Cable had over 30 million subscribers nationally. In 1988 it was the fourth-largest cable network in the country and Robertson officially changed the network's name to the Family Channel. Robertson had gone from a successful religious broadcaster to one of the major cable network operators.

Meanwhile, the percentage of religious broadcasts on CBN Cable declined in spite of the amazing popularity of Robertson's own news and feature program, "The 700 Club," which attracted more viewers every month than any other religious television show. The success of "The 700 Club" may have led Robertson to overestimate his potential as a presidential candidate. In any case, when he left the show to run for the Republican nomination in 1987, audience ratings and contributions plummetted. Moreover, his move into politics proved ill-timed, coinciding with the televangelism scandals which greatly lowered public confidence in religious broadcasters. Robertson's return to "The 700 Club" after his unsuccessful bid, however, bailed out the financially strapped network.

The Jim and Tammy Show

Bakker's program was a combination of self-help philosophy, variety show, personal soap opera, and charismatic worship. Where one of these left off and another began was often difficult to predict. Like much charismatic worship, "The PTL Club" was highly emotional and frequently spontaneous. "The 700 Club" normally consisted of scripted discussions and well-edited segments taped in advance, whereas Bakker's broadcast frequently followed the whims of the host. Ultimately this helped insure Bakker's fall, for he sometimes invented new fund-raising projects and audience appeals in the middle of an emotional outburst about the plight of the ministry.

Bakker's own rise to celebrity status was his personal testimony to the veracity of the Christian faith and to the truth of his own version of it. No one could challenge his success in worldly terms: luxurious clothing, expensive automobiles, numerous homes. His life mirrored the promises he claimed for his audience. Like the theology of the old-fashioned Pentecostalism he was nurtured in as a child, Bakker's philosophy was highly experiential.

Bakker created the major religious cable network called the "PTL Network" or "The Inspirational Network." Most local cable operators would only carry one religious network, and Bakker grabbed the spot before other religious broadcasters had learned how the cable industry was run. Over 13 million Americans subscribed to Bakker's network by 1986, although far fewer watched "The PTL Club" or its successor, "The Jim and Tammy Show." Bakker was never able to attract large audiences, but his viewers were among the most loyal in religious broadcasting. Bakker sold time on the channel to other religious broadcasters, including other Pentecostals, thereby subsidizing the costs of his own satellite system and program production.

Always an incredibly talented television fund raiser, Bakker had an uncanny ability to elicit contributions by tugging on the heart strings of viewers. His most successful technique was to offer viewers "time shares" in motels constructed on the grounds of his Heritage U.S.A. religious theme park near Charlotte, North Carolina. In only a decade, Heritage U.S.A.'s attendance climbed to third among theme parks in the United States behind only the two Disney parks. Bakker left the network in the hands of Baptist televangelist Jerry Falwell in 1987, after admitting he had sexual relations with a church secretary years earlier. However, Falwell found it impossible to run his own ministry and PTL at the same time. Months later he turned PTL over to professional managers who hoped to bail it out of bankruptcy without the help of Bakker's fund raising.

Televised health and wealth

The most controversial offshoot of traditional Pentecostalism to enter the airways is the so-called health-and-wealth gospel, also called the "faith movement" and "name it–claim it" religion. Like the messages of so many broadcast preachers, the faith movement is market driven. It not only holds that divine healing takes place in the world today, but that healing and prosperity are guaranteed to all Christians who have adequate faith. In other words, the fruits of the gospel depend upon the believer's "positive confession," his acting as if he has already received his special blessings from God. Believers must "claim" their healing or financial inheritance. If they do not claim it, they do not receive it; God gives to those who have the greatest faith.

The faith movement is a particularly American phenomenon that has been accelerated by the power of mass media to transmit new ideas quickly to large, impersonal audiences. It is animated by the superstitious elements of American society evidenced in supermarket tabloids, lottery games, and various marketing schemes trumpeted through the mail and in the classified section of some popular magazines. It offers the kind of hope that people want to have, and teaches what many people want to believe, and it claims to emulate the miraculous setting of the New Testament church—a desire that has always appealed to Pentecostals.

Kenneth Copeland, the movement's rising television star, effectively captures on his "Believer's Voice of Victory" program the Pentecostal sense of the immanence of God. He prophesies and occasionally speaks in tongues on the air; more important, he claims divinely inspired insight into the Scriptures, adding his own wisdom to the Word of God. In addition, Copeland preaches and sings with the vocal style and physical movement of a nightclub performer. His young audience is evidence that he might be the first Pentecostal television evangelist in a long while to build an influential, long-term ministry, like Roberts did in the 1950s.

Spontaneity over scripting
Two things have always marked Pentecostal broadcasting: spontaneity and emotional appeals. As history would have it, these were also well-known formulas for successful broadcast programs. Partly because of its theological roots, and partly because of its cultural style, Pentecostalism and the electronic media gravitated toward each other.

Theologically, Pentecostalism's "second blessing" upon the individual believer was powerfully dramatic. Tongues speaking and slayings in the Spirit were entertaining, especially compared with the emotionally languid rituals of many other evangelical traditions. Few Protestants could top baptism in the Holy Spirit as a powerful media presentation; even the forgiveness of sins, in spite of its biblical foundation, was boring programming. Moreover, Spirit baptism and divine healing captured exciting manifestations of God's apparent entry into human lives. Pentecostals did not merely preach about God; they displayed evidence of God. That was more than most Christian programs could offer; as long as Pentecostal broadcasters clipped off the fringe practices of their faith and cast the programming in mainstream evangelical terms, they could hardly go wrong on the tube, except for growing competition.

Culturally speaking, Pentecostals generally followed the oral communication styles of preindustrial societies. In a nation where mass communication was increasingly routinized and standardized, Pentecostal programs were an attractive alternative. Pentecostal cultures were animated by the spontaneous power of the spoken word, not the carefully planned logic of the scripted page. Even into the 1980s, the programs of new-style Pentecostals such as Jim Bakker and old-fashioned Pentecostals such as Jimmy Swaggart conveyed spontaneous excitement compared with the vast majority of religious broadcasting. Each of their shows was a unique "event" that, like the spoken word in an oral culture, could never be completely recaptured. Eventually audio- and videotape captured this spontaneity for later transmission, but the power of such messages was barely diminished. Like the revival tent, the airways were a "live" medium that carried real voices and images. Even if the program were recorded, the sounds and sights seemingly mirrored the actions of actual people, not merely the impersonal words of a printing press.

But for all of its natural affinity for the microphone and the camera, Pentecostalism could rarely let loose the power of its "full gospel." Electronic equipment and air time had to be supported financially through the contributions of large audiences. Pentecostals adopted their message to the rising consumer culture they once hoped to convert to their own gospel. As a result, Pentecostal broadcasting became a smorgasbord of entertainment and preaching, histrionics and teaching, increasingly shaped by the health-and-wealth gospel and the charismatic movement.

Fine tuning for the future

In the late 1980s, the boom in Pentecostal broadcasting was stalled by a flurry of major and minor scandals among some of the prominent televangelists. Roberts claimed in 1987 that the Lord would "call him home" if his ministry was unable to raise $8 million for medical-student scholarships at Oral Roberts University. A race-track owner in Florida saved the televangelist at the last minute with a seven-figure donation, but Roberts's ministry suffered immeasurably from what some observers called "holy extortion."

During the same period, Jim and Tammy Bakker left the PTL ministry amid news reports that Jim had seduced a church secretary years earlier and that the ministry had paid hush money to the victim. Soon a host of other charges about the Bakkers' misuse of ministry funds and about other sexual misconduct at PTL severed the Bakkers from their own organization. Fundamentalist Baptist Jerry Falwell ran PTL for a time, but the long-term financial health of PTL looked increasingly dismal as the ministry lost its theme park near Charlotte and struggled to survive bankruptcy proceedings.

Clearly the biggest blow, however, to Pentecostal broadcasting came in 1988 when top-rated weekly televangelist Jimmy Swaggart stepped down from the pulpit for six months amid numerous charges about his visits to an area of prostitution along a highway between New Orleans and Baton Rouge. Although few of the charges were ever proven, Swaggart tearfully confessed on his program to his own "sinfulness" and called upon supporters to forgive him. It appeared that Swaggart might come through the scandal relatively unscathed, but he refused to abide by the disciplinary guidelines of his own denomination, the Assemblies of God, which recommended at least a year's suspension from the pulpit. Realizing the consequences of a year-long silence for his top-rated television ministry, Swaggart defied the AOG and resigned his ministerial credentials, hoping to build a completely independent ministry. The result was a cloud of public skepticism about Swaggart's repentance, which seemingly had been orchestrated so effectively on the tube. To many people inside and outside of Christianity, Swaggart's brand of emotional TV revivalism was now highly suspect.

On top of everything else, Robertson's bid for the Republican presidential nomination in 1988 revealed additional cracks in the credibility of Pentecostal broadcasting. Several news media reported that Robertson's earlier autobiography had been rewritten to eliminate the section where God had once told the evangelist that Christian ministers should not run for public office. Also, the liberal People for the American Way distributed videotapes of some of Robertson's earlier activities on "The 700 Club," including his claim that his ministry "prayed away" a hurricane from the southeast coast of the United States.

Worst of all for Robertson, he repeatedly denied that he was ever a television "evangelist," preferring the term "religious broadcaster." Clearly Robertson was attempting to separate himself from the scandalous world of televangelism. As he blasted the news media for their "religious bigotry," however, his public credibility diminished. After losing miserably even in southern primaries, Robertson eventually faced his own political fallout and returned to his faltering CBN Network and the floundering "The 700 Club," which in Pat's absence was hosted by his less-dynamic son.

In the end, the image of Pentecostal broadcasting in the United States greatly suffered as a result of the misdeeds and misguided actions of a few well-known figures. That's all it takes in television, where images are created and destroyed overnight, and where the roads to popularity often follow perilous curves and dangerous cliffs to self-destruction. If television greatly popularized Pentecostalism in the 1970s and early 1980s, it also tarnished the image of Pentecostalism in the late 1980s. Television giveth and television taketh away. It remains to be seen whether the scandals will have any long-term effect on Pentecostalism, but at least in the short run, they undoubtedly will slow the progress of Pentecostal broadcasting.

Chapter 8

NEW CULTURES. NEW CHALLENGES. NEW CHURCH?

L. Grant McClung, Jr.

"I am inclined to think that if Pentecostals would stress signs and wonders in the ethnic community, they could win them in a big way."
—Donald A. McGavran

From the beginning, Pentecostals have been a strange breed, locked in a time warp between the past and the future. When supernatural phenomena burst on the scene at the turn of the century, Pentecostals were sure they were living in the end-time restoration of New Testament apostolic power. Signs and wonders were a portent of Christ's imminent return. Little wonder, then, that "the movement" took off with such explosive dynamism. Pentecostals simply put everything else aside and got on with the business of world evangelization.

To catch the dimensions of this "vision" as it has made an impact on international Pentecostalism today, consider the following statistics from David B. Barrett's annual update, "The 20th Century Pentecostal/Charismatic Renewal in The Holy Spirit, With Its Goal of World Evangelization" (*International Bulletin of Missionary Research*, July 1988):*

- 332 million affiliated church members worldwide;
- 19 million new members a year;
- 54,000 new members a day;
- $34 billion annually donated to Christian causes;
- Active in 80 percent of the world's 3,300 large metropolises;
- 66 percent of membership in the Third World.

Barrett's cross section of worldwide Pentecostalism reveals a composite "international Pentecostal" who is more urban than rural, more female than male, more Third World (66 percent) than Western world (32 percent), more impoverished (87 percent) than affluent (13 percent), more family oriented than individualistic, and is younger than eighteen.

As Barrett notes, at the heart of issues and trends that must be addressed are the "sheer magnitude and diversity" of the renewal and (in this writer's estimation) the alarming dissimilarity between Barrett's international composite and the North American WASP ("White Anglo-Saxon Protestant," or in the case of my own southeastern-bound denomination, "White Anglo Southern Pentecostal"), middle-class Pentecostal. Moreover, the rapid influx of ethnic Pentecostals from overseas into North America, combined with the center of Pentecostal initiative and vitality moving away from older European and North American–based (and controlled) organizations, calls for a reevaluation and restrategizing of Pentecostal missiology.

In short, we have entered a new era.

The globe at a glance

Western Europe: Though not experiencing the same proportions of phenomenal growth as the Pentecostals in "Latfricasia" (Donald McGavran's collective term for Latin America, Africa, and Asia),

---

*Included in these statistics are evangelicals who exercise the gifts of the Holy Spirit without identifying themselves as either Pentecostal or charismatic. Categorized as "Third Wavers" by C. Peter Wagner, they numbered twenty million in 1988.

European Pentecostalism has nonetheless had some encouraging developments, many in the last ten years.

Scandinavian Pentecostals have led the way in missions, communication (electronic and print media), and in incorporating the Pentecostal message into indigenous church structures. The well-known Filadelfia Church in Stockholm has grown to seven thousand members. Pentecostal missionaries make up one-half of all Scandinavian missionaries, with main concentrations in Africa and Brazil. And Swedish Pentecostals have close to 850 missionaries in forty-eight countries.

Their counterparts in Great Britain and on the European continent have continued their efforts through new-church planting, literature distribution, the establishment of Bible schools, and the development of parachurch ministries such as Teen Challenge and Youth With A Mission.

The changing ethnicity characteristic in North American cities has also brought a corresponding pluralism to much of Western Europe. In England, for example, the most rapid Pentecostal growth has been among West Indian immigrants. In Brussels, the fastest-growing congregation in all of Belgium draws from the more than 15 thousand African immigrants from Zaire. The Church of God (Cleveland, Tenn.) congregation there grew from a handful in 1986 to more than eight hundred in 1988, drawing most of its membership from Zaire's professional class. The pastor and elders pray for eight hours prior to the two o'clock Sunday afternoon service, at which time healings and exorcisms are common.

Eastern Europe: Though the recent political atmosphere of *glasnost* has brought the spotlight once again to Eastern Europe, a Pentecostal church has been steady and burgeoning there for years. This is the result of Pentecostal penetration since the early 1900s and the more recent charismatic renewal in the historic churches.

Romania, with more than two hundred thousand Pentecostal believers, has been marked with explosive growth, earning the church-growth reputation as "the Korea of Europe." The recently formed Pentecostal church in Poland claims some ten thousand members in eight-six local churches, making it the largest of the five groups composing the Evangelical United Church of the Gospel.

Unlike the stereotype of aging, persecuted Christian believers huddled together in secret gatherings, a leading Hungarian sociologist, Miklos Tomka, notes that "the church in Hungary is full of young people, and they worship openly." The Soviet Union's official youth movement, Komsomol, reported a loss of two million members in the first eight months of 1988. At the same time, observers are reporting a measurable increase in church attendance by young people. Indeed, the European Pentecostal movement is a *youth* movement, both East and West.

Seminars, theological education by extension, and other creative forms of leadership training are also growing among Eastern European Pentecostals. The Biblical Theological Institute in Yugoslavia has some fifty resident students from nine nationalities. With an additional two hundred extension students, this Assemblies of God college is the largest evangelical training school in Eastern Europe. And the school's president, Peter Kuzmic, is perhaps the first Pentecostal to serve as the chairman of the theology working group of the World Evangelical Fellowship.

Ministerial training and distinctive Pentecostal theologizing have also been advanced through EPTA, the European Pentecostal Theological Association. EPTA has brought together a wide network of European Pentecostal Bible schools and scholars. The association publishes the *EPTA Bulletin* and has initiated a feasibility study for a European Pentecostal seminary.

Africa and the Middle East: The Christian movement as a whole is growing too rapidly in this varied region to chart or analyze completely. C. Peter Wagner has noted that the Christian population south of the Sahara will have grown from ten million in 1900 to a projected 400 million by the year 2000. This will raise the proportion of Christians, he says, from 8 to 50 percent.

Pentecostals and charismatics certainly have their share in this revival. Though many thriving ministries were planted and mentored by expatriate Pentecostal missionaries (mainly from the U.S., Canada, and Europe), much of the recent growth has been from African independent churches. In recent times, says Wagner, new indigenous African denominations have been forming at the rate of one per day!

Africa has produced "mega ministries" such as Reinhard Bonnke's Christ for All Nations crusades, which regularly attract tens of thousands. The closing rally of his June 1988 crusade drew an estimated two hundred thousand and was broadcast live throughout Kenya over radio and television. Across the continent in West Africa, Pastor Benson Idahosa has constructed a 20 thousand–seat sanctuary in Benin City, Nigeria. His fellow Nigerian, William Kumuyi, has seen his weekly Bible study grow from fifteen people in 1973 to 26 thousand in 1988. At the same time his main congregation was averaging 56 thousand believers. Bonnke, Idahosa, and Kumuyi would all cite the ministry of the Holy Spirit in demonstrated power as the primary reason for their success.

In South Africa, the Pentecostal/charismatic alternative represents a major force for change. The Pentecostal movement is expected to be the strongest religious movement there by the year 2000. The Apostolic Faith Mission is establishing some one hundred new congregations annually. Groups such as the Full Gospel Church of God (more than 200 thousand strong) are creating new models of multiethnic cooperation and leadership. And a recent resolution from the Fellowship of Pentecostal Churches has stated that group's opposition to the government position of apartheid, ruling the practice unbiblical.

The Muslim dominance of the African Sahara in the North remains a challenge to Pentecostals as well as all evangelicals. Though such ministries as Lillian Trasher's social work among Cairo's orphaned and homeless children are exemplary, no wide-scale success has been found among Pentecostals in North Africa or in the Middle East.

Historically, much of the American and European Pentecostal indifference to Muslim evangelism has been the result of a premillennial preoccupation with the nation of Israel and other topics related to prophecy. Dwight J. Wilson notes, for example, that "A flurry of apocalyptic interest accompanied World War II. In the first three months of 1941, thirty-one out of ninety major articles in the Assemblies of God *Pentecostal Evangel* were about prophecy and the war in Europe." (See Wilson's article on "Pentecostal Perspectives on Eschatology," in the *Dictionary of Pentecostal and Charismatic Movements* and his *Armageddon Now! The Premillenarian Response to Russia and Israel Since 1917*, Baker Books, 1977.)

However, the Assemblies of God are to be credited with a renewed sense of responsibility to the Muslim world. Their creative strategies in the Middle East, along with their Center for Ministry to Muslims in Minneapolis, Minnesota, are creating new models of outreach to Muslims. In addition, the presence of more than two hundred thousand Pentecostals in Indonesia, the world's largest Muslim nation, presents new opportunities for evangelism. One movement there, the Bethel Church of God, has set an optimistic goal of ten thousand new churches by the year 2000.

Asia: Churches that are designated Pentecostal, charismatic, or that exhibit Pentecostal styles of worship and ministry (prayer for the sick, exorcisms, etc.) are clearly emerging as the "new Antiochs" of Asia. One such church is Singapore's Calvary Charismatic Center. In just ten years the church has grown to more than five thousand members, has a $1.2 million missions program, and has sent more than two hundred witnesses on short-term church-planting teams.

Across the South China Sea from Singapore, the Philippines enjoys one of the most exciting revivals in modern church history, and Pentecostals are right in the middle. One of them is Church of God missionary Gerald Holloway, who started a Bible study in his living room in the early 1980s. Eight years later he was pastoring a burgeoning congregation of more than ten thousand members, with branch congregations among the Filipino diaspora in Singapore, Australia, Hong Kong, and Southern California.

Of course, the church-growth scene in Asia is dominated by Korea's Paul Yonggi Cho and his superchurch of five hundred thousand members on Seoul's Yoido island. To the west, mainland China's 50 to 80 million Christian believers are largely typified by ministry practices associated with Pentecostal/charismatic theology and method.

And in Japan, charismatic and Pentecostal fellowships flourish. In Tokyo, Cho's daughter congregation numbered three hundred members in 1987. In the same year, the local Church of God had more than fifty adult conversions—considered remarkable growth in Japan.

Australia and Oceania: A wide variety of evangelical denominations used the recent bicentennial celebrations in Australia as an opportunity to challenge the nation's spiritual decline and present the gospel. While several mainline denominations have plateaued or declined, Pentecostal/charismatic churches showed an astounding

Decadal Growth Rate (DGR) of 385 percent from 1976 to 1981. The second-highest figure was reported by both the Catholics and the Baptists—a 24 percent DGR.

More incredible, perhaps, is the fact that during the first forty years of the Assemblies of God in Australia (1937–77), the denomination grew to only 152 congregations with 9,446 members and adherents. Yet during the next ten years (1977–87), the denomination jumped to 550 churches, 950 ministers, and approximately 85,000 members and adherents. Today the Assemblies are reaching for one new congregation in every town with a population of over a thousand people.

Latin America and the Caribbean: Latin American evangelicalism and Pentecostalism are virtually synonymous. Some observers feel that as high a ratio as three of every four evangelicals are Pentecostal. According to World Council of Churches spokesman Eugene Stockwell:

• About 66 percent of the three million Protestants in Mexico are Pentecostals (compared to no Pentecostals among the 21,000 Protestants in Mexico in 1916).

• The overwhelming majority of Protestants in Nicaragua are Pentecostal—estimates vary from 60 to 80 percent.

• In Chile, between 80 and 90 percent of the Protestants are Pentecostal.

To these statistics, veteran church watcher C. Peter Wagner has added:

• In thirteen of the twenty major Latin American republics, a Pentecostal denomination was the largest of the Protestant groups reported in 1985.

• Two of the three largest churches in the world are in Latin America, and both are Pentecostal.

In short, in spite of monumental challenges such as urbanization and political turmoil, Latin American Pentecostalism has developed into a model movement in terms of contextualization, theology, polity, evangelism, and social action.

The reality of ethnic America

The international political turmoil of the sixties and seventies, combined with relaxed immigration laws in the U.S., brought about a massive new wave of overseas immigration and resulted in a new "ethnic America." This reality was addressed at the historic National Convocation on Evangelizing Ethnic America in Houston, Texas, in 1985. Pentecostals were key players in the planning and execution of Houston '85—little surprise since "ethnic evangelism" has been integral to their identity and character from the outset.

As Everett A. Wilson notes, ethnic diversity was notable at the Azusa Street revival. Pentecostals did not have to form a cross-cultural outreach to a minority group since they themselves were the urban ethnic poor. Hispanics, Europeans, and American blacks and whites all worshiped God together and were endowed with charismatic manifestations.

"Mexicans were present at Azusa Street," claims historian Roberts Mapes Anderson. Within ten years after the Azusa Street revival (1906–09), "Pentecostal preachers of Spanish extraction," says Anderson, "had firmly planted Pentecost among the 'floating population' of migrant Mexicans in many cities and towns from San Jose to Los Angeles to San Diego and throughout the outlying farm areas."

Today one-half of the Southern California District of the International Church of the Foursquare Gospel is ethnic, reaching out to Iranians, Armenians, Taiwanese, Hispanics, and blacks. In the famous Angelus Temple, where flamboyant Aimee Semple McPherson electrified large Anglo audiences, a congregation of 1,500 Hispanics worships.

However, the changing complexion of American Pentecostalism is not solely an urban phenomenon. In New England, for example, small-town Pentecostal congregations teach English to Cambodian refugees; in Dalton, Georgia, a thriving church reaches out to transplanted Mexicans working in carpet mills; near Lodge Grass, Montana, Church of God state overseer Dan Boling has an open door to share Christ with an aging Crow tribal chieftan, his entire tribal council, and another 150 tribal leaders.

Following the general pattern in ethnic evangelism, most of the thriving ethnic churches are homogeneous congregations, speaking the same language, coming from the same culture. Many, however, such as Robert Hinson's intercultural Church of God congregation in Reading, Pennsylvania, or the Arlington, Virginia, Assemblies of God, have developed as multiethnic congregations. The Arlington congregation, mostly Hispanic, has 450 members representing over forty-five nationalities. The worship services are integrated with translation transmitters provided for those needing interpretation. Pastor Richard Neubauer says that up to 40 percent of the budget is designated for missions work.

A number of ex-Muslims attend the church, where works of the Holy Spirit are freely encouraged. In one encounter, an Iranian woman came forward during Neubauer's altar call and exclaimed, "Jesus!" The deacons reported later that the woman had not understood the sermon. However, when the pastor bowed for prayer, she saw Jesus standing beside him and cried out. Immediately she went on to win her three sisters to the Lord.

The "internal" challenges of ethnic diversity
The great diversity of Pentecostal church families around the world, and the scattered mosaic of Pentecostal ethnics now in the U.S., will present major challenges in the 1990s and ultimately reshape the appearance of American Pentecostalism in the twenty-first century. These challenges can best be described as "internal issues" (those within the ethnic Pentecostal communities themselves) and "external issues" (those touching the interrelationship between ethnic churches and older Anglo Pentecostals).

There are four major internal issues within the ethnic community facing North American Pentecostalism today.

1. *Leadership hierarchies versus the voice of the people.* Many of the ethnic churches come from highly structured, "vertical" societies in which a clear power structure maintains senior leadership and tends to hold back younger, emerging leaders. Thus senior ethnic leaders who complain of being closed out of decision-making and leadership processes in Anglo circles may themselves be limiting the involvement of their own younger leaders. It is only a matter of time until this "frustrated" generation turns to other denominations, parachurch organizations, or starts independent ministries of its own.

2. *The move toward respectability.* John Root's study of West Indian Pentecostalism in Great Britain found that as immigrant poor congregations were captivated by middle-class values and status symbols, their evangelistic success began to wane. "Nothing

puts a greater question mark against the future of West Indian Pentecostalism," he claimed, "than the temptation for material success to sever them from their roots in the black community." The same peril looms over ethnic Pentecostals in North America who would follow their Anglo middle-class brothers and sisters down the path of "health and wealth" and, in the process, upgrade themselves toward social and evangelistic irrelevance. Internal discrimination in ethnic communities toward those with FOB status ("Fresh Off the Boat") is an open secret. Evangelistic effectiveness may be at stake if ethnic Pentecostals move closer to becoming carbon copies of their WASP counterparts.

3. *Privatization versus community.* The family nature and sense of community in ethnic Pentecostal churches is a hidden treasure longed for in many cold and static Anglo congregations. Ethnic Pentecostals will need to guard against the encroachment of the American glorification of the self-made person. The pull for prosperity and material success is strong among the ethnic newcomers.

Along with this concern, ethnic churches will need to avoid an inward vision that works against a world vision. Preoccupation with their own survival can blur the vision for a wider participation in the global cause of Christ. Though not always embraced and welcomed by Anglo Pentecostals, ethnic Pentecostals cannot afford to separate their vitality and contributions from wider church bodies. As their strength increases, so will their temptation toward segregation and fragmentation.

4. *Second-generation cooling of spiritual fervor.* Many ethnic congregations are struggling to maintain their Americanized youth. To compound the challenge, an aggressive "reevangelization" campaign is now being launched by other religions and sects. Muslim mosques and social centers dot the American landscape, not only seeking new converts but "harboring" incoming Muslims for the faith. The largest Buddhist temple in the Western hemisphere rises like a monolith just outside Los Angeles in suburban Hacienda Heights. This is no accident since the largest concentration of Asians outside Asia is in Southern California.

An alarming number of American blacks are not only being influenced by Islam but are turning to such sects as the Jehovah's Witnesses. And at key entry points in the nation, Mormons sponsor "welcome centers" for disoriented refugees, offering jobs, housing, and English as a second language (ESL) programs. Ethnic Pentecostal leaders need to be reminded that "the empire will strike back."

The "external" challenges of ethnic diversity

Some of the external issues related to the interrelationship of emerging ethnic Pentecostals and their North American counterparts are best placed in context by reviewing David Barrett's composite "international Pentecostal" mentioned earlier and remembering the prophetic observations of Anne Parsons made in "The Pentecostal Immigrants: A Study of An Ethnic Central City Church" (*Practical Anthropology*, November–December, 1967). Wrote Parsons: "At the present time, middle-class Protestantism has little or no relation to the working-class Protestantism embodied in the very different ethnic churches and small store-front sects."

And speaking of ethnic Pentecostal congregations, she continued: "But one of the sad facts about such movements of the Spirit today is that they are almost completely unknown to the Protestant residents of American suburbs. These latter are indeed introverted, in that their religious energy is either focused only on private life, or it is directed toward the refinement of subtle sectarian differences based on consumption in a world in which material tokens of the Lord's favor have no more meaning because there are too many already."

Today, WASP Pentecostals have "moved uptown," joining the ranks of respectable, suburban Protestants. And like proverbial "ships in the night," North American Anglo Pentecostals and their ethnic brothers are passing each other, in spite of promotional brochures from denominational departments of intercultural ministries and token appointments of "ethnic brethren" on boards and committees.

Consequently, what I fear is the development of a "two-tiered class structure" in American Pentecostalism that plays out some of the following issues.

1. *Issues of accountability and representation.* When *Time* magazine referred to Latin American and Hispanic American church growth as "the fastest growing church in the hemisphere" (Nov. 2, 1962), they were recognizing a movement that could result in the "Hispanicization" of American Pentecostalism. The sad fact is that a

generation has passed since the *Time* observation, and many ethnic leaders are still asking when their "time" will come in terms of full participation and representation in the structure to which they have demonstrated loyalty and accountability.

2. *Issues of culture, location, and economics.* Ethnic Pentecostals are increasingly representing a "counter culture Pentecostalism" that was characteristic of pre-World War II American Pentecostalism. On the other hand, Anglo Pentecostalism has become captive to culture, buying into American civil religion, "Kingdom Now" theology, and the gospel of prosperity. Both Anglo and ethnic churches must return to a "sojourner strategy" and "pilgrim proclamation."

Black Pentecostals have been characterized by black church leader J. Alfred Smith, Sr., as "The Invisible Church" (*Christianity Today*, Mar. 3, 1989). One of the reasons why black churches and those of their other ethnic brethren are not seen is that, for the most part, WASP Pentecostals have fled to suburbia while ethnic Pentecostals have stayed largely in the city. Hispanics, for example, are overwhelmingly an urban population, with half found in metropolitan inner cities. This creates a scenario in which the crying social issues faced by urban ethnic Pentecostals remain largely ignored by their WASP brethren. Pentecostal evangelism must once again be coupled with wholistic concerns.

3. *Issues of theology and polity.* The Anglo theology of human government, with its corresponding issues of nationalism versus patriotism, is viewed differently by our new Pentecostal neighbors from Eastern Europe and the Soviet Union. Newly arriving Latin American Pentecostals are giving their North American brethren lessons in liberation theology. And others in the ethnic community are ordaining women while some American Pentecostal clergymen struggle with this option. Both groups need to discuss openly questions of distinctives and doctrines in the light of Scripture and under the guidance of the Holy Spirit.

Strategies for the next century

Virtually every mainline Pentecostal group in America has set ambitious goals to reach by the year 2000. The Assemblies of God has its "Decade of Harvest" evangelism thrust; the Church of God (Cleveland, Tenn.) has "Project 2000"; the Pentecostal Holiness

Church has adopted "Target 2000"; and the International Church of The Foursquare Gospel has projected "2,000 Before 2000" (a domestic church-planting effort).

But the challenges that cause us to forge new strategies are common challenges to both Anglo and ethnic Pentecostals. Thus, to face the future, these two communities must join together for a fourfold advance:

1. *To move into new fields.* Barrett's claim that Pentecostals/charismatics are now active in 80 percent of the world's 3,300 metropolises is an encouraging, strategic opportunity. But this is basically a non-Western, non-Anglo statistic. Thus the future rebuilding of American cities lies in the hands of the ethnic community. Therefore, new partnerships combining the manpower and financial resources of both segments in North American Pentecostalism need to be forged if this physical *and* spiritual rebuilding is to be realized.

2. *To reach new "target" groups.* The parameters of our mission can no longer be put into simple regional or geographic categories. Pentecostals, along with all evangelicals committed to the Great Commission, need to restructure their categories and reshape their target audiences. For example, we are facing the reality of one billion urban squatters within ten years—men, women, and children scratching out a meager "living" in a world where 80 percent of the global population exists on less than $650 per year. And it is a young harvest, with 40 percent of the world's citizens under eighteen years of age.

The "upper economic tier" of North American Anglo Pentecostals are philosophically and geographically isolated from the majority of the target audience just described. Yet they continue to control the lion's share of the financial resources. On the other hand, ethnic Pentecostals in America may have a ready lifestyle and mindset to match the needs of the new target audiences. Partnerships must be formed to reach these target groups.

3. *To actively train professionals and laypeople alike.* There are at least seven types of evangelizers needed in the immediate future of Pentecostal missions: world-traveling laity, short-term professionals, the newly retired (second-career people), pastors with a world parish, career missionaries from Western churches (North American/European), overseas missionaries from overseas churches, and

an international network of Christian students.

The "new personnel" in missions will involve the financial resources of overseas churches who will not only evangelize non-Western regions but also send missionaries to the ethnic populations of North America and Europe. In the Church of God (Cleveland, Tenn.), for example, Japanese and German members give more per capita to world evangelization than their American counterparts.

Denominational mission boards and parachurch missions agencies in North America will also need to learn to live with new types of networking relationships: for example, superchurch to superchurch as opposed to U.S. denominational missions departments to national church leadership. In this relationship pastors will be key players. Anglo church leaders in denominational judicatories (states, conferences, districts) will also need to work with the realities of close networks between rapidly growing ethnic churches and strong overseas national movements. In these relationships, North American Pentecostal leaders should be developing partners, not protégés.

There is unparalleled opportunity for ethnic American Pentecostalism to play a critical role in international missions. How many "Daniel Bergs" are there among the Asian, European, Hispanic, Pacific Island, and West Indian Pentecostal churches in America today? Berg and another lay companion left as Spirit-baptized laymen from Chicago in the early 1920s to found the Pentecostal movement in Brazil. Today that massive country has the largest Assemblies of God constituency on earth—some nine million adherents and sixty-seven thousand national ministers.

4. *To reawaken believers to the power of the Holy Spirit.* It is naïve to think that ethnic Pentecostal churches are the only depository of dynamic spirituality. WASP Pentecostals, however, must face the fact of their own waning spiritual ardor and learn from their ethnic brethren.

With a growing historical reference and signs of advancing institutionalization, Anglo Pentecostalism is at a watershed so aptly discussed in Margaret Poloma's sociological survey, *The Assemblies of God at the Crossroads: Charisma and Institutional Dilemmas* (University of Tennessee Press, 1989):

... despite the verbal support I have found given to charisma, I also see a growing alignment with the successful evangelical denominations, many of which deny the validity of Pentecostal experiences, and a refusal to cooperate with mainstream charismatics who share a Pentecostal ideology. These observations have implications for the future of the institution and the fate of charisma within the institutional walls.

Mainline North American Pentecostalism is in danger of succumbing to a secular world view in which the supernatural is given lip service but is not a factor in daily living. In this regard, the ethnic Pentecostals may, in the long run, hold the key to revitalization. Donald McGavran observed in the early 1980s that most ethnic newcomers to this country are not yet secularized, holding a supernatural world view. "I am inclined to think that if Pentecostals would stress signs and wonders in the ethnic community, they could win them in a big way," he said.

In reality, as Anglo Pentecostals intersect with, and humbly learn from, their ethnic fellow travelers, they themselves will be won in a big way. And the future advancement of North American Pentecostalism will be assured.

Chapter 9

MAINTAINING DISTINCTIVES: THE FUTURE OF PENTECOSTALISM

Russell P. Spittler

Pentecostals hardly realize what has become of their movement. By July 1989, David B. Barrett's updated figures showed fully 351 million Christians could be reckoned as Pentecostals or charismatics of one sort or another. That figure actually exceeds the number of Protestants in the world—who total 318 million. (This excludes the 53 million Anglicans who don't call themselves Protestants.)

The values, beliefs, and practices of Pentecostals have spilled over into the larger world of Christianity. In fact, *Pentecostalism can now be viewed as the second most widespread variety of Christian spiritual lifestyle*—after the globally uniform liturgy of the Mass practiced by 944 million Roman Catholics, who make up more than half of the world's 1.72 billion Christians. This Pentecostal/charismatic lifestyle marks, to use Barrett's mid-1988 figures, 10 percent of the world's Anglicans, 12 percent of all Roman Catholics, and 65 percent of all Protestants. What this means is that Pentecostal and charismatic spirituality cannot be compressed into that cluster of denominations and charismatic groups that salute the Azusa Street flag. It is still true that the Spirit blows where he wills.

A Christian renewal movement with this breadth of influence—one now completing a century of history—approaches the twenty-first century with a clear set of tensions, challenges, and threats.

Twin perils: Triumphalism and elitism

University of Chicago church historian Martin Marty once observed that Pentecostals used to argue God's approval upon them because they numbered so few. But more recently, he said, the proof has shifted to the fact there are so many. More than ever before, the twin threats of triumphalism and elitism are poised to tempt the movement—dazzled by its own rapid growth and rising influence—into a self-congratulatory trance.

Triumphalism describes a sometimes subtle pattern of group chauvinism, a stance—as one wordcrafter put it—of "rusting on one's laurels." The older and more organized Pentecostal bodies are less inclined toward this diversionary decadence than burgeoning charismatic megachurches—though they might have even more warrant to celebrate.

There is one noticeable redeeming factor for some (but not all) of the older established Pentecostal bodies, such as the Church of God (Cleveland, Tenn.) and the Assemblies of God. It lies in the fact that in these groups there is no single honored human founder of the church—no John Wesley or John Calvin, no Martin Luther or Menno Simons—some might add no Mary Baker Eddy or William Miller. These groups in fact honor the Holy Spirit instead of a celebrated founder. As one banner headline put it in one of the daily conference newspapers for the seventy-fifth anniversary general council of the Assemblies of God held in Indianapolis during the summer of 1989, the Holy Spirit is "the Hero of the Harvest." Such a focus on the Holy Spirit often has the effect of redirecting the triumphalist impulse toward the Trinity.

Elitism, however, is more difficult to evade. An implication of spiritual superiority inadvertently emerges, primarily from the tenacity of Pentecostal commitment to its distinctive "initial evidence" doctrine—the belief that the postconversional baptism in the Holy Spirit has not occurred unless it is accompanied by the evidence of speaking in tongues, as recorded in Acts 2:4.

The originators of this belief, which goes back at least to Charles Parham's Topeka Bible school and the year 1900, were not intending at the time to comment upon the spiritual quality of the religious experience of others. Rather, they were looking to upgrade their own spirituality. But when relentless Western logic is applied, as certainly happens in the North American fundamentalist-evangelical environment, a necessary logical consequence arises: Anyone who does *not* speak in tongues has not received the baptism in the Spirit. Non-Pentecostals feel that makes them second-class citizens.

As is already true in certain German, Scandinavian, and South American Pentecostal bodies, the elitist implications of an unrelenting initial evidence position may be reduced by the mere switch from "the" to "a": speaking in tongues *may be a consequence* of the Spirit's personal coming rather than *will be the initial physical evidence.* This softer outlook, indeed, already constitutes on the North American scene one of the conspicuous contrasts between the charismatic movement and its classical Pentecostal forbears. Charismatics overall allow, but don't require, glossolalic evidence.

Some emerging classical Pentecostal scholars understandably rejoice in the widespread acceptance of "their beliefs" in wide sectors of the church. No clearer evidence of that parochial success can be cited than the emergence of what Fuller Seminary church-growth specialist C. Peter Wagner has dubbed "the Third Wave"— the adoption within mainline and evangelical churches of such Pentecostal beliefs and practices as prayer for the sick, laying on of hands, words of knowledge, prophesying, and speaking in tongues.

Yet, Third Wavers, who were reckoned by David Barrett to exceed 28 million by mid-1988, find no reason to leave their evangelical and mainline denominations. Nor do they speak of themselves as Pentecostals or charismatics—classical, denominational, or otherwise.

Most evangelical multidenominational seminaries these days welcome Pentecostal and charismatic students, and at one of them, Gordon-Conwell Theological Seminary, Pentecostal scholar Robert

E. Cooley serves as president. At Fuller Theological Seminary in Pasadena, the combined totals of Pentecostal and charismatically inclined students reaches nearly 50 percent of the student body. But not all schools are that receptive. Dallas Theological Seminary in 1988 released three professors thought to have been unduly influenced by the free charismatic expression in corporate worship advocated by John Wimber's Vineyard Fellowship. For all the ecclesial friendliness with Pentecostals, stiff pockets of opposition survive. With the stylized image of an ominous serpent both on the cover and on an inside double-page spread—unmistakenly reflecting the biblical image of Satan—a 1986 book from the Religious Right strongly warns against deception by *The Pied Piper of the Pentecostal Movement.* Any sort of gleeful triumphalism among Pentecostals would therefore be both premature and blind indeed, let alone of questionable ethical warrant.

If any temptation persists toward undue horn blowing, Pentecostals may have to take note of the fact that it is not they but the Mormons who are the fastest-growing American religion. And tucked away on page 23 of one of its daily conference newspapers was a brief paragraph reporting the 1988 Sunday morning average attendance in the Assemblies of God as 1,451,065—down 22,091 from 1987 (the second consecutive year of a decline). Clearly, there is no room for complacency.

Pentecostal/charismatic relations

Outsiders see them as similar, but classical Pentecostals by no means embrace uncritically everything that goes by the name *charismatic.* At one of the World Pentecostal Conferences in the early 1970s, one enthusiastic attender introduced himself to the conference chair T. F. Zimmerman as a charismatic Christian Scientist! Say what you will about institutionalization and ecclesiastical structures, if functioning properly, they clarify doctrine and stand guard against heretical teaching.

The conspicuous difference between Pentecostals and charismatics lies in how, in their times, they were received by their home churches. For the most part, Pentecostals in the early 1900s were not welcomed back into the mainline fold. Charismatics, overall, stayed loyal to their churches (although everyone hears of conspicuous exceptions). Virtually every major variety of Protestantism has its "charismatic service committee" that works hard to interpret the charismatic impulse to the unsure majority and domesticate it for those who identify with the revival. Barrett's 1988 count of 21 million denominational charismatics among the 332.7 million Pentecostal and charismatic church members had no counterpart at this century's beginning.

Some leaders of the established Pentecostal bodies expect the charismatics, sooner or later, to find a church home in Pentecostal congregations. Many do. But the majority stay loyal to their own church and are often instruments of renewal in the mainstream of Christianity.

Besides, classical Pentecostals (at least in North America) very jealously guard their distinctive doctrine of initial evidence, while charismatics widely decline to make that commitment. These realities suggest that in the next century Pentecostalism will continue to preserve its hard-won identity and dispense—with great success—its variety of lively Christian piety.

But the charismatic movement will likely continue to flourish more as a renewing lifestyle than as an institutionalizing body, awakening nominal Christians, rekindling piety, and spiraling off toward reabsorption into the churches. The stunning phenomenon of the Third Wave shows a clear trend in this direction. Pentecostalism has become institutionalized: the charismatics are dominantly a movement. Can anyone cite a widely known Christian denominational group with "charismatic" in its name?

Church slowth

Still another intriguing facet of the global situation among Pentecostals and charismatics discovered by David Barrett concerns "post-Pentecostals" and "postcharismatics." Barrett's research showed 2.6 million "post-Pentecostals" and 80.7 million "postcharismatics" (27.4 million Protestants, 53.3 million Roman Catholics). The phenomenon specially occurs among Roman Catholic charismatics, among whom there are roughly five postcharismatics for each of the 10.1 million currently active Catholic charismatics.

Of course, there have always been ex-Pentecostals who write sensational books like *I Once Spoke in Tongues*. To this day there has been no thorough sociological analysis of the reasons why former Pentecostal ministers leave the church and what accounts for similar shifts out of Pentecostal congregations. We study the front door—church growth. Why not the back? *(Church slowth?)*

I know from endless talks with Pentecostal students over three decades that the core beliefs of their church—its distinctive beliefs about baptism in the Holy Spirit—are the subjects of much reflection. To a great extent, this happens because the exegetical, theological, and even historical supporting research for these beliefs is so scant. Pentecostalism is a largely anti-intellectual tradition where personal experience counts often for more than reasoned exegesis. The more substantial theological material comes from better equipped charismatic scholars, and very few of their words would pass muster in Pentecostal precincts.

Academic dilemmas like these faced by today's seminarians—whether in multidenominational seminaries or in Pentecostal graduate schools—often lead to a shift in denominations.

But even if Pentecostal ministerial students were to find theological satisfaction, post-Pentecostalism will abound. To be frank, Pentecostals are often better at making new Christians than nurturing old ones. This trait was illustrated when, at its 1989 general council, the Assemblies of God considered a proposal to enfold into a combined organizational unit the educational work of the church—ranging from Sunday schools, Christian day schools, institutes, colleges, and the graduate seminary—with an accompanying suggestion to explore establishment of a university. A national executive director over this educational thrust would be paralleled organizationally only by the executive director of the mission enterprise. The motion, which gave the appearance of lofting evangelism and education as the twin works of the Church, was not approved; it was referred to an enlarged committee. Such an action may have been the right one, but it shows as well that evangelism and education were not created equal in the eyes of one major classical Pentecostal body—a view probably typical of other bodies as well.

Pentecostal education and scholarship

Still, basic schooling in Scripture and evangelism has been a hallmark of classical Pentecostalism. But only since World War II have Pentecostal educational enterprises widened to include college education for those not entering ministry. And only since the Vietnam War have there been Pentecostal seminaries. Interestingly, the first Pentecostal seminary, Atlanta's Charles H. Mason Theological Seminary, founded in 1970 by the mostly black Church of God in Christ, is still the only one that carries full seminary accreditation. Hopes for a seminary jointly sponsored by the major Pentecostal bodies have not materialized: denominational interests understandably prevail. And the checkered history of other Pentecostal graduate schools (California Theological Seminary (Fresno), CBN University, Jimmy Swaggart Theological Seminary, Melodyland School of Theology, Oral Roberts University) teaches the wisdom of sufficient planning not merely for continual funding but for a well-conceived design of what these schools will do and—especially— whom they will serve. The time is not too far distant when a pan-Pentecostal conference on graduate educational strategies may be in order.

There is a surprising scramble through the final quarter of this century among Pentecostal ministers for doctoral degrees of any sort. All too often among the academic *nouveau riche* who have had no substantial academic tradition, one doctorate looks the same as any other. In California, honorary doctorates from unaccredited schools have been bestowed upon pastors in Sunday evening services. One local church operates a seminary offering Th.D.'s and D.Min.'s, citing unsought "international accreditation" by an agency since put out of business by a state governmental sting operation.

On the other hand, in 1990 the Society for Pentecostal Studies observed the conclusion of its first twenty years. About six-hundred scholars, teachers, pastors, leaders, and authors are members. An annual meeting, a twice-yearly theological journal, and a few published works yield collective evidence of advancing academic maturity. Pentecostal scholars increasingly show up on faculties of secular universities as well as in evangelical and denominational seminaries in Canada, Europe, and the United States. If charismatic scholars are included, hardly a continent is left untouched.

The most substantial theological publication arises from Roman Catholic charismatic scholars: J. M. Ford, Donald Gelpi, Peter Hocken, Kilian McDonnell, Heribert Mühlen, Francis Sullivan, and

Simon Tugwell. Following, somewhat less in literary productivity, come Protestant charismatic scholars Howard Ervin, Henry Lederle, and J. Rodman Williams. Just concluding a distinguished academic career as an observer of global Pentecostalism is Swiss scholar Walter Hollenweger, perhaps the most voluminous analyst of Pentecostalism and himself a post-Pentecostal of sorts.

Some of classical Pentecostalism's most astute published scholars teach in Canadian schools—Gordon Fee (Regent College), Larry Hurtado (University of Manitoba), and Gerald Sheppard (Emmanuel College in Toronto). A host of younger classical Pentecostal scholars are emerging in North America, and among the brightest are several European Pentecostal scholars (whose polylingual abilities let them easily include the vast resources in German and French). The arrival of the twenty-first century will see the first major theological works to emerge from classical Pentecostalism: I expect those writings to come at first from the Europeans but eventually from Latins, Africans, and Asians.

Dealing with ecumenical impulses

According to Joel 2:28, the Spirit was to be poured out upon "all flesh." And this verse has become something of a battle cry for globe-girdling Pentecostals. Yet the inevitable process of institutionalization—what German sociologist Max Weber called "the routinization of charisma"—has had a curious reversing effect. If it is right to describe Pentecostalism as fundamentally a spiritual lifestyle, only rejoicing among Pentecostals should accompany its increasing acceptance. Not so. Ecumenical efforts are looked upon by many Pentecostal leaders as the blind leading the blind toward an unattainable and undesirable goal. The hesitance is proper, certainly, where ecumenical ambitions have sought a unified church at any theological cost. There is, however, an ecumenism of personal interchange, and for that the charismatic impulse is well suited.

North American Pentecostals acquire a number of their attitudes from the fundamentalist-liberal conflicts of the 1920s—a battle in which they themselves had no real part. The Pentecostal outbreak in the early 1900s addressed individual spiritual needs. Fundamentalist protests were more matters of the head than of the heart, rational theological protests to the intellectual drift in Western Christianity.

Before the Second World War, American Pentecostals were themselves objects of fundamentalist scorn. After the war, Pentecostals became evangelicalized. It therefore seems right to say that the North American Pentecostal establishment learned to oppose global ecumenical developments from their fundamentalist and evangelical siblings.

Around 1960, the Assemblies of God's chief executive officer was also president of the National Association of Evangelicals; and the evangelicalization of Pentecostalism was well under way. It was naturally a considerable embarrassment, then, when Assemblies clergyman David du Plessis found increasing acceptance in churchly quarters traditionally regarded as liberal. (He was defrocked in 1962, but reinstated in 1980.) Du Plessis' support for unitive movements found him involved in such cross-denominational agencies as the World Pentecostal Conference, the Pentecostal Fellowship of North America, and the Full Gospel Businessmen's Fellowship International. His most influential role, however, was to serve as co-chair of the International Roman Catholic–Pentecostal Dialogue, the first session of which began in 1972.

The Catholic–Pentecostal Dialogue, which completed its third five-year cycle in 1989, represents the deepest involvement of Pentecostals in ecumenical affairs. The dialogue teams, generally six to ten on each side, have enlarged the mutual understanding of the churches. Pentecostal church leaders understandably had to distance themselves from such activities, given the widespread belief among Pentecostal students of biblical prophecy that Rome was the Great Harlot of the Book of Revelation, coupled with isolated yet sharp local Roman Catholic hostility toward Pentecostal missionizing.

However, recent members of the Pentecostal Dialogue teams have had the concurrence, or at least the acquiescence, of their church leaders. These younger participants are often university trained, quite able in theological dialogue. And they keep their superiors fully informed.

As an outcome of such dialogue, some national ecumenical talks have emerged. Fuller Seminary's David du Plessis Center for Spirituality has, along with the National Council of Churches, cosponsored an ongoing Consultation on Pentecostalism. Highly involved in all these ecumenical activities is Cecil M. Robeck, Jr.—whom

Walter Hollenweger once described as "a sort of academic David du Plessis." Robeck, an Assemblies of God minister, teaches church history and is an associate dean at Fuller Seminary.

It is not yet clear just what participation, if any, classical Pentecostalism will have when the Seventh Assembly of the World Council of Churches convenes in February 1991 in Canberra, Australia. If Pentecostals are not present, it won't be for lack of interest in the announced theme: "Come Holy Spirit—Renew the Whole Creation."

Surely a major challenge in the coming decades for Pentecostals lies in balancing an uncompromising witness in unusual places with avoidance of past isolationism. Quiet participation in ecumenical discussion could allow just that.

Laying Elmer Gantry to rest

The ghost of Elmer Gantry "reappeared" with the public moral crash in 1987–88 of two major Pentecostal televangelists. Though it would not be anyone's chosen way to come into public view, the Assemblies of God managed both the Jim Bakker and the Jimmy Swaggart affairs in a temperate and even-handed manner that drew wide acclaim.

Moral failure in the ministry is as old as Judas, and perhaps we snould not be surprised if the average reaches one in twelve, as it did in Jesus' band. Among David Barrett's assorted numbers, however, appears a startling rise in ecclesiastical crime. From 1980 to 1989, embezzled ecclesiastical funds leaped from $80 million to $762.5 million.

Over the coming decades, Pentecostals will have to outlive the Elmer Gantry image. In a society shot through with ethical decay, the lofty value put on personal religious experience will require the counterbalance of simple virtues. Charisma is no good without character. The fruit of the Spirit rate equal time—rather, more time—than the gifts of the Spirit. Tongues will cease, but love goes on forever.

Too little holiness, too much freedom?

In 1988, national attention was focused on the Church of God (Cleveland, Tenn.) when it voted to lift long-standing bans against certain hair styles, use of cosmetics, and the wearing of wedding bands. To some of the older saints, this appeared as a compromise to founding principles. To other observers, it came off as a welcome recognition that holiness is more a matter of the heart than the hair.

The real test will come in how well the Church of God rank and file can make this slight shift without going overboard. Legisated holiness has long characterized the Pentecostals, especially those most directly descended from nineteenth-century forebears in the holiness movement. A sturdy challenge faces Pentecostals in the new freedom: can they, and especially their children, move into a mature, self-disciplined interior holiness? Can they endure freedom?

Accommodation is the term sociologists of religion use to describe how aging renewal groups fit themselves to changing culture. In her major study, *The Assemblies of God at the Crossroads* (University of Tennessee Press, 1989), University of Akron sociologist Margaret Poloma—herself a Roman Catholic charismatic—concluded that the largest Pentecostal body presents a classic study in the routinization of charisma. Although the Assemblies of God is organized "well beyond the interest of its founders," it demonstrates overall (she says) a healthy mix of charisma and bureaucracy.

The health of the denomination, as well as its pace-setting growth rate among sister churches, may be attributable to its unique combination of presbyterial and congregational governing styles. The strong sense of local-church sovereignty in the Assemblies of God counterbalances the leveling effect of national organizational regulation. The local pastor holds the key role, and he (they are usually male) may be forgiven some stylistic or doctrinal peculiarities because of the strong power base in a local congregation.

As Pentecostalism reaches toward its second century, accommodative forces no doubt will continue the exchange of charisma for routine. Bureaucracy will increase, the bylaws expand. But Margaret Poloma rightfully observes that the shift from charisma to organization need not be all that inevitable nor as pessimistic as the patriarchal German sociologist Max Weber made it out to be. There is room for hope.

Charles Darwin and tongues speaking

What is distinctive is not necessarily what is quintessential: Consider how much more than stripes are zebras, the American flag, and the barber pole. Pentecostalism's doctrinal origin came when the biblical phenomenon of speaking in tongues was described as the necessary initial physical evidence in the Holy Spirit.

Increasingly through the nineteenth century, holiness churches and others developed a belief in the need for the baptism in the Holy Spirit as the empowering and sanctifying experience available to believers and hence subsequent to conversion. Various "evidences" had been proffered—visible emotion, enhanced capacity for witness, deeper love for the Bible, among others. Pentecostals, struck by the precedents in Acts, declared glossolalia as the necessary sign.

An invisible cultural undercurrent might have played a role here. In 1859 Charles Darwin published his *Origin of the Species*, popularizing from fossil evidence the notion of human evolution. Higher criticism, mostly imported from Germany, similarly announced jarring conclusions based on historical "evidence." Conservatives demurred, but could it be that they were subtly captured by the *method* of what they opposed? That each fact must have its "evidence"? Is this how, in the generation after the Civil War, earnest Christians came to look for the "evidence" of the baptism in the Spirit? The word "evidence" does not appear in Acts, and partly on that account Pentecostals have had little success in persuading others, including the majority of their charismatic cousins, to accept the belief.

But if the initial evidence doctrine made little headway among outsiders, the Pentecostals took it as their most characteristic "distinctive." If others have doubts, they have redoubled efforts to maintain the distinctive. When some charismatics reported receiving the Spirit but not speaking in tongues until months later, the Assemblies of God issued reinforcing clarification to the effect that no one receives the baptism in the Holy Spirit unless and until glossolalic evidence accompanies.

Classical Pentecostals will not easily modify this view. Consequently, it will be difficult for Pentecostals to avoid the charge of an isolative elitism. But the past three decades have shown something of an arms-length truce with the evangelical establishment. Both have found kind words for each other, and they cooperate without acrimony in common causes.

Candidates for Pentecostal ministry *must* have spoken in tongues, and Margaret Poloma found that 69 percent of her sampling of pastors in the Assemblies of God did so daily. But glossolalia occurs less frequently among the Pentecostal rank and file. Though three-fourths of her respondents attested a personal baptism in the Holy Spirit, 11 percent of those went on to say they had never spoken in tongues. A *Christianity Today* Gallup Poll conducted in 1979 found that only 17 percent of persons who considered themselves Pentecostal or charismatic also said they had *ever* spoken in tongues. The practice is not as widespread as the movement it characterizes.

It may well be time to move away from polemics over the evidence of the Spirit's coming and to focus rather on the outcome. Foursquare pastor Jack Hayford, in fact, proposed at Lausanne II in Manila (1989) use of the term *pleromatic* rather than *charismatic* or even *Pentecostal*. Stemming from the Greek word for fullness, the term has the promise of transcending the politics of churchly adjectives of all sorts. And it describes a completeness sought by earnest Christians everywhere. That could be the idea of the decade.

Hence, Pentecostalism has become a firmly established variety of twentieth-century Christianity. It may be, as Prof. Donald Dayton suggests, "the most influential Christian tradition of our time." Forces of institutionalization clearly affect the older established denominations, but these have not stunted its rapid growth. The balanced institutionalizing process finds illustration in emergence, amid a tradition squarely committed to "divine healing," of ministry to the blind and the deaf, and, a recent development, the rise of medical ministries—hospitals, nurses, and physicians included.

The charismatic movement may indeed have "peaked," but not before 30 million adult Roman Catholics were renewed and 65 percent of all Protestants in 1989 drew from its resources. Movements are more shapeless than established denominations. The charismatic impulse is a strong one, and no doubt there are more seamy schismatic chapters in church history to come. The turn of the new century will bring with it the ready means for manufactured religious experience—spiritual highs on demand. But more than experience is needed.

The Pentecostal tradition deeply values personal religious experience. Its first century has shown a capacity to contain that experience, to direct it toward community growth and even social betterment. That would not have happened without some degree of institutionalization. Still maintaining its distinctives, the movement forges ahead under its accustomed banner—"Not by might, nor by power, but by my Spirit, saith the Lord."

Conclusion

A SENSE OF DESTINY

Harold B. Smith

Over the years, I've had numerous opportunities to discuss Pentecostalism—its up sides and down sides—with the men and women whose energies are all consumed in giving the movement leadership. One such exchange remains particularly fresh—prophetic, even.

The date was March 1987—just two months before *Bakker* became a household word. I was on assignment for *Christianity Today* magazine and had scheduled separate interviews with Bishop Leon Stewart of the International Pentecostal Holiness Church, Ray H. Hughes of the Church of God (Cleveland, Tenn.), Ray Smith of the Open Bible Standard Church, and G. Raymond Carlson of the Assemblies of God. We discussed distinctives, the charismatic movement, and doctrines in light of the Pentecostal agenda for the twenty-first century.

Challenge one: Distinctives

Each man maintained that a primary challenge facing the whole of Pentecostalism related to its distinctives: the doctrine of the baptism of the Holy Spirit and the subsequent gifts of healing and speaking in tongues. Ironically, these "tell-tale signs" have been perceived by many *within* Pentecostalism as a mixed blessing—a regrettable stumbling block to closer relationships with non-Pentecostal denominations, yet a heaven-sent stepping stone for bringing tens of thousands to a saving knowledge of Jesus Christ.

Today, however, the tendency to downplay distinctives is clearly on the outs. Or, as the soft-spoken Ray Carlson said, "If we don't hold our distinctives, what's the use of our existing?"

According to Ray Smith, "power" Pentecostalism was temporarily subdued in an effort to be more sophisticated. "There was the desire to be accepted," Smith said, "to flow into the evangelical community and not be considered an offbeat movement. Now I see us moving back to a freer expression of life in Jesus—in ways a little more common and acceptable—but without sacrificing our distinctives."

Such talk comes out of a movement that no longer sees identification with non-Pentecostal groups as an essential step toward winning respect from the broader religious community (although Pentecostals clearly appreciate that wider identity). The movement has gained respect, if only because it is one of the largest groupings under the evangelical rubric.

Ray Hughes, a Bible scholar and articulate Pentecostal spokesman, described his own denomination—the oldest within classic Pentecostalism—as "a lively group" still drawing objections from the more staid wing of evangelicalism because of its distinctives. Nevertheless, said Hughes, it is a group where "the gospel is on fire, rather than on ice." The same could be said for the other three denominations as well.

"The emphasis on experience, on being built on the Holy Spirit, on being alive," added Smith, "is like a love relationship where there's emotion flowing and deep commitment, rather than a businesslike relationship solidly based on marriage principles alone. Pentecostalism adds the zip."

And it is this characteristic "zip" that Pentecostals recognize as their peculiar kingdom contribution, and that is an attraction to

more and more people. "The presentation of the real Jesus in our everyday lives and in our worship services," said Bishop Stewart, "will attract a lot of people to our church."

"It [the baptism of the Holy Spirit] is not our main doctrine," cautioned Carlson. "That, of course, is Christ crucified, resurrected at the right hand of the Father. Still, it's important to maintain the Pentecostal distinctives."

"I think Pentecostals probably feel pretty comfortable with where they are," said Smith. "It's the non-Pentecostal evangelicals who are less and less comfortable—and they have to deal with that."

Challenge two: Charismatics

Coming out of the closet with their distinctives will also necessitate Pentecostals continuing to come to terms with the charismatic movement. As we have already seen, surface similarities between classic Pentecostals and charismatics belie deep doctrinal differences. Thus, what looks to be a ready-made reservoir of new members for the historic Pentecostal churches is, in fact, a fiercely independent group within mainline Protestant and Catholic churches whose freedom earmarks both its worship style and doctrine. That troubles many Pentecostal leaders.

"I'm grateful for what the charismatic movement has brought with regard to celebration," commented Carlson. "But it seems to be steeped in a very humanistic, materialistic kind of orientation. We need more than celebration. We need that balance of the Word and the Spirit. We need to anchor solidly in the Word of God."

Said Hughes: "We just do not endorse doctrines like positive confession—you know, 'name it–claim it,' 'confess it–possess it.' People are going to do that and be disappointed. But then again, I can hope those people go back to study the Scriptures concerning asking and having. They'll see there are instructions, limitations. It says if he abides in you and if his words abide in you, and if it's according to his will. From this closer inspection, and a desire to grow, they will come to the established Pentecostal churches. I am positive of that."

Indeed, providing charismatics an anchor in the historic Pentecostal denominations is one way to minimize the "name it–claim it" aberrations.

"The independent movements," continued Hughes, "are beginning to look for roots. They are looking for a solid place, a solid base—something they can sink their teeth into and raise their families in."

Challenge three: Doctrine

Of course, some of the doctrinal excesses of the charismatic movement have mirrored similar excesses within the historic Pentecostal churches and have consequently served to warn the older movement against biblical infidelity. The age-old challenge to shore up emotionalism with a solid theological framework remains the quintessential question facing Pentecostal leaders today.

"If you are living on experience only, you're going to run aground," Hughes said. "You must have an experience based in the Word, and not simply on whatever kind of theological framework you want."

Clearly a concern of all the men was the materialistic prosperity gospel, trumpeted most noticeably by Pentecostal televangelists—even after Bakker. Their comments concerning this "false witness" were particularly interesting in light of the fact that they were made prior to the PTL revelations.

"American churches have to get rid of hypocrisy, showmanship, sensationalism—a lot of that stuff," said Bishop Stewart. "The young people today are smart enough to see right through that. What they want is the real Jesus."

"It's so easy to be caught up in 'me-tooism'—what's in it for me," Carlson said. "We are not to use the Holy Spirit, the Holy Spirit is to use us. We must ask ourselves if what we are doing is just for us or for God's glory. You can't just name it and claim it."

Explained Hughes: "Most of us Pentecostals came from the blue-collar working class, and the thing that made the movement grow was that it brought the gospel to the poor. We must not forget that, regardless of how the gospel has lifted us materially. We must not let materialism dominate us."

"I like to put it this way," Carlson added. "Stay in the middle of the streams of divine truth. Don't be carried away by some of the spectacular. We can claim by faith, but the extremes—that's what I want us to be careful of."

In the end, back to basics

Carlson's "middle of the stream" analogy summarized the general direction each of the four men hopes to steer his respective denomination in the days ahead. While seeing Pentecostalism as unique, they all revel in that uniqueness only as it clearly focuses on a biblical understanding of man's sinfulness, God's love and forgiveness, and life in Christ.

"We have a threefold goal," Carlson said. "First, that there would be a renewal of a sense of the holiness and the majesty of God. There's an intimacy we can experience. We should draw near to him in prayer. He's not far off."

"Second," Carlson continued, "I pray that God would give our people a burning passion for the lost. And finally, I ask that God would give us a sense of discipleship with the spirit of servanthood."

When I first heard that agenda two years ago, it sounded like standard religious fare. But time has shown that agenda to be anything but standard. Three hundred million adherents—and growing—are hard to ignore. Little wonder an exuberant Ray Smith triumphantly exclaimed near the end of our interview that Pentecostals have a sense of destiny "because Pentecostalism is biblical."

Appendix 1

GROWING UP PENTECOSTAL

James R. Goff, Jr.

T hough the "Holy Roller" stigma was much greater for the first two generations, Pentecostal baby boomers like me learned at an early age that their church was different from mainline churches. Revivals came frequently—at least once each quarter. Generally scheduled for a week or ten days, these events could easily stretch into an additional week if the evangelist sparked the proper emotional surge. Since there was a special virtue in attending every service, revivals forced children to get their homework done early, miss regular television programs, and keep late hours. If a service was particularly successful with a lot of "lingering around the altar," young people would fall asleep in the pews before the service ended. The next morning, memories of being carried gently from the church, taken home in the car, and undressed for bed merged with the night's dreams.

Revivals, camp meeting and youth camp every summer, occasional Friday night sings, and the regularly scheduled Sunday morning, Sunday evening, and Wednesday evening services meant a great deal of time in church. Some of my earliest memories are of Mr. Johnny running down the aisle, Brother Westbrook shouting "Glory," and my mother speaking in tongues. These displays signaled the arrival of Holy Spirit power, and, even as a child, I understood that those moments symbolized that all was well with the church. They occurred frequently enough to shock no one, but infrequently enough to draw the special attention of us kids. We might even giggle at the demonstrations, though we were compelled to avoid the notice of parents. In time, the displays would take on new significance as youth revivals and adolescence brought us into the worship style.

The emotional content of worship services provided a potential source of ridicule from non-Pentecostal friends. I remember being very anxious when friends visited church with me—secretly hoping that a "dry" service would be the order of the day.

Restrictive patterns of behavior marked Pentecostal youth even more vividly. Strictures against movies, make-up, dances, gym shorts, and playing ball on Sunday alienated faithful Pentecostal youth from their peers and caused tensions with parents determined to enforce such measures to the letter. Some of the conflicts were no different from those experienced by all parents and their children; Pentecostal youth simply faced more of them more often. In addition, their choices were portrayed in concrete religious terms; one could choose God and family or friends and popularity.

A religious inferiority complex
Identifying yourself as Pentecostal was traumatic if you were particularly self-conscious of the value judgments of others. Sometimes you could mask the trauma by displaying excessive zeal. Pentecostalism became a cross to bear; the taunting and ribbing, a badge of your rightness with God. At other times, the response was not nearly so heroic.

Entering the religion program at Wake Forest University as a junior-college transfer, I faced an experience that demonstrated the latent embarrassment embedded in youth reared in churches less than socially acceptable. Having fought a stuttering problem since childhood, I prided myself on having overcome any notice of the handicap by practicing restraint in my speech patterns to avoid embarrassing mental blocks. In an interview with the dean of the religion department, however, the malady struck with full force in an encounter I will never forget.

The dean casually asked what denomination I belonged to; and there in the midst of a bastion of Southern Baptist respectability, I suddenly forgot how to talk. Or rather, I could not say the two crucial words *Pentecostal Holiness.* "I'm . . . ah. I belong to the . . . ah. It's the . . . ah. . . ." Seconds seemed like hours as I gave a perfect rendition of a college religion major who somehow forgot the name of his own church.

For a brief moment I considered passing myself off as Baptist or Methodist. Even Presbyterian. Those names seemed easy to say. Finally, the dean interrupted, "Well, that's okay. It's not important." But I persisted. "No, I can say it. Just a moment." His interruption had broken the spell, and a second later I managed to sputter, "I'm Pentecostal Holiness."

Our conversation continued, and though I was never sure exactly what the dean thought of the strange episode, the timing convinced me that I suffered from a religious inferiority complex. Sure I had stuttered, stammered, and faced mental blocks before, but never at such a crucial moment when faith itself seemed on the line. I was embarrassed at myself, and yet proud that at least I had persisted. The episode revealed my desire for responsibility—not respectability gained by jumping ship, but rather by somehow making *Pentecostal* a term respectable in itself.

It was never again quite so hard to say "Pentecostal Holiness"; I had come to accept my feelings of inadequacy and recognized my need to overcome them.

Old struggles, new struggles

In recent years, Pentecostalism has lost much of its stigma. Enormous growth and the rise of the charismatic movement have broadened the scope of knowledge about Pentecostals and given added prestige to churches once located only on the "other side of the tracks." The road promises to be much different for future generations of Pentecostals, and the tensions that I felt so keenly have decreased—and should continue to do so.

However, new tensions will surely take their place as Pentecostals face a question formerly addressed to other religious organizations striving for the mainstream: Can Pentecostals remain Pentecostals in an environment of respectability, or will the unique quality that fostered strength be lost?

Appendix 2

PENTECOSTALISM "REINVENTED": THE CHARISMATIC RENEWAL

J. I. Packer

The charismatic movement, also called the renewal movement and the charismatic renewal, is a worldwide phenomenon about thirty years old. Some refer to it as the second Pentecostal wave, in distinction from the first wave that produced the Pentecostal denominations at the start of this century. It emerged in California, as did its predecessor, and has touched most Christian bodies, including the Roman Catholic community. Pentecostals are relatively unaffected, but that is natural since, from their standpoint, charismatic renewal is just the rest of the church catching up with what they themselves have known for two generations.

The charismatic movement has spread far and fast. Approximately 25 million Christians outside the Pentecostal churches have adopted a recognizably charismatic approach to Christian and church life.

What is that approach? It is a matter of embracing some, if not all, of the following items:

1. A hermeneutical claim that all elements of New Testament ministry and experience may with propriety be hoped for, sought, and expected today, none of them having permanently ceased when the apostolic age ended.

2. An empirical claim that among the elements of New Testament ministry and experience now enjoyed within the renewal are: (a) experiential postconversion Spirit-baptism, as seen in Acts 2:1–4; 8:14–17; 10:44–46; with 11:15–17; 19:1–6; (b) tongues, understood as *glossolalia* (uttering languagelike sounds) rather than *xenolalia* (speaking languages one never learned) and as given primarily for private devotional use; (c) interpretation of tongues, when spoken in public; (d) prophecy, understood as receiving and relaying messages directly from God; (e) miraculous healing through prayer; (f) deliverance from demonic influences through exorcism; and (g) words of knowledge, understood as supernatural disclosings of information about individuals to those who seek to minister to their needs.

3. A high valuation of one's own glossolalia as a personal prayer language, and deliberate, frequent use of it.

4. Emphasis on the church as the body of Christ, upheld and led on to maturity by the Holy Spirit through the mutual love and supernaturally empowered service of its members.

5. A concern to identify and harness each Christian's spiritual gift or gifts for body ministry.

6. Insistence that worship is central in the church's common life, and that the heart and climax of true worship is united praise as distinct from preaching and Eucharist (which have been the historic focal centers of Protestant and Roman Catholic worship respectively).

7. The cultivation of a relaxed, leisurely, intimate, informal style of corporate worship, aimed at evoking feelings of awe and joy before the Lord and at expressing love and loyalty to him for his saving grace.

8. The use for this purpose of simple, repetitive choruses and "renewal songs," often consisting of biblical texts set to music in a modern folk idiom for performance with guitar accompaniment. Guitars may be reinforced by melody instruments and also by tambourines, bongos, and jazz drums, as in a dance band's rhythm section.

9. The congregational practice of "singing in the Spirit"—that is, sustaining ad lib, and moving within, the full-close chord with which a hymn or song ends, vocalizing extemporarily and sometimes glossolalically in the process.

10. Encouragement of physical expression of the spirit of praise and prayer by raising hands, swinging the body, dancing, prostrating oneself, and other such gestures. Bodily movements of this kind are held to deepen worship by intensifying the mood being expressed, and thus to glorify God.

11. Expectation of prophecy in worship gatherings, either as an immediate, on-the-spot message from God or as the remembered fruit of a vision or a dream, and the provision of opportunity to utter it to the congregation.

12. The typical perception of people both outside and inside the community of faith less as guilty sinners than as moral, spiritual, and emotional cripples, scarred, soured, and desperately needing deliverance from bondages in their inner lives; and the structuring of counseling and prayer ministries to meet their need, thus viewed.

13. The practice of prayer with laying on of hands, for all who desire it, as a regular conclusion to worship gatherings. Those who are sick, disabled, and troubled in mind are particularly urged to receive this ministry and to expect benefit through it.

14. A counseling technique of leading pained, grieved, inhibited, and embittered souls to visualize Christ and involve him therapeutically in the reliving of their traumatic hurts, as a means to inner healing.

15. A confident assumption that it is not ordinarily God's will that any of his children should continue in pain, or in any mental and emotional state other than joy, and a consequent downplaying of the older Christian stress on the spiritual benefit of humbly accepted suffering.

16. An insistent claim that miraculous-looking "signs and wonders" (especially "healings") have evidential value that will convince modern Westerners of the truth and power of the gospel, and that "signs and wonders" should therefore be sought from God by prayer in each congregation.

17. A firm belief that some, if not all, disturbed people with addictive enslavements (bondages) are under the influence of

demons who must be detected and exorcised.

18. A commitment to aggressive evangelism, aimed at inducing the self-willed to repent and open their lives to Jesus Christ and his Holy Spirit.

19. Emphasis on the benefit of communal and community living; of prayerfully sharing all one's concerns with "the body," normally in small groups, and of accepting discipline and guidance from other Christians in authoritative mentor relationships.

20. Insistence that established patterns of personal and church life must always be open to change so that Holy Spirit life may find freer expression, and expectation that all Christians, fellowships, and congregations will need to make such change over and over again.

21. Expectant openness to divine guidance by prophecy, vision, and dreams.

22. Confidence that a shared charismatic experience and lifestyle unifies Protestants and Roman Catholics at a deeper level than that at which doctrine divides them.

23. A devotional temper of exuberant euphoria, expressing a sense of loving intimacy with the Father and the Son that has in it little self-assessment and self-criticism, but is affectionate and adoring in a happily childlike way.

The movement in perspective

Evaluation of this kaleidoscope phenomenon needs to be made from a number of angles.

Sociologically, the charismatic movement is a restrained, white, middle-class reinvention of original working-class, black-style, "Holy Roller" Pentecostalism, from which it has borrowed much of its theology. Its relative uninhibitedness frequently approaches, but rarely transgresses, the bounds of educated good taste.

Spiritually, it is a recognizable mutation of the Bible-based conversionist piety fostered in seventeenth-century Puritanism, in New England's Great Awakening, and in the nineteenth-century Protestant missionary movement—the type of piety that is nowadays labeled "evangelical." Original Pentecostalism was an adaptation of this piety in its Wesleyan form, but Calvinistic charismatics are currently found in some strength.

Doctrinally, the renewal is in the mainstream of historic evangelical orthodoxy on the Trinity, the Incarnation, the objectivity of Christ's atonement and the historicity of his resurrection, the need of regeneration by the Holy Spirit, personal fellowship with the Father and the Son as central to the life of faith, and the divine truth of the Bible. There is nothing eccentric about its basic teaching.

Theologically, charismaticism is a mixed bag, as witnesses this perceptive vignette by Richard Lovelace:

> The charismatic renewal continues to express the mystical spirituality of the Puritan and awakening eras, but often without the rational and theological checks against error and credulity maintained by evangelicals. As a consequence, charismatics have some of the problems of the radical spiritualists in the anabaptist and Puritan left wing. Gifts of the Spirit are more prominent than the call to sanctification. The charismatic garden has a luxuriant overgrowth of theological weeds, including the health-and-wealth gospel, the most virulent form of the American heresy that Christianity guarantees worldly success. A fuzzy and unstructured ecumenism lives side by side with rampant sectarianism ("Evangelical Spirituality: A Church Historian's Perspective," *Journal of the Evangelical Theological Society* 31, no. 1 [March 1988], p. 33).

Granted, the renewal has an enviable track record of enlivening the spiritually dead and energizing the spiritually paralyzed, but whether it commands the resources to lead them on to full-orbed Christian maturity is another matter. When the liturgical and pastoral innovations that initially channel the new life become routines as stylized as those they replaced, and the limitations listed by Lovelace are accepted as normal, is not some writing beginning to appear on the wall? And the question, How may the renewal be renewed? does not seem to have been faced as yet, let alone answered.

For an expanded review and evaluation of the charismatic movement, see Dr. Packer's chapter "Is the Charismatic Renewal, Seen in Many Churches Today, of God?" in Tough Questions Christians Ask *(Victor Books, 1989), pp. 47–60.*

ABOUT THE AUTHORS

Gordon L. Anderson *is associate professor of ancient studies at North Central Bible College, Minneapolis, Minnesota. He also directs the G. Raymond Carlson Institute for Church Leadership. Anderson is a graduate of Southern California College, the University of Portland, and the University of Minnesota, where he received his Ph.D. in ancient studies.*

James R. Goff, Jr., *is assistant professor of history at Appalachian State University, Boone, North Carolina. He is a graduate of Emmanuel College, Wake Forest University, Duke University, and the University of Arkansas. His doctoral dissertation on Charles Parham and the missionary origins of Pentecostalism was developed under the direction of David E. Harrell, Jr., and was published by the University of Arkansas.*

L. Grant McClung, Jr., *travels and writes from his home base in Cleveland, Tennessee, where he is associate professor of missions and church growth at the Church of God School of Theology. He is the contributor of Pentecostal missiology to the* Dictionary of Pentecostal and Charismatic Movements *(Zondervan, 1988), and is visiting lecturer on church growth at Fuller Theological Seminary School of World Mission*

David Edwin Harrell, Jr., *is University Scholar at the University of Alabama. He holds degrees from David Lipscomb College and Vanderbilt University (M.A., Ph.D.). He has written six books on American religious history, including two recent biographies:* Oral Roberts: An American Life *(Indiana University Press, 1985) and* Pat Robertson: A Personal, Religious, and Political Portrait *(Harper & Row, 1987). Widely recognized as an authority on evangelicalism and religion in the American South, Harrell has appeared on such national television programs as "Good Morning, America," "Nightline," "CBS News," and "CNN News."*

William W. Menzies *is currently a missionary with the American Assemblies of God, serving as president of the Far East Advanced School of Theology in Baguio, Philippines. He is a graduate of Central Bible College, Wheaton College, and the University of Iowa, where he received his doctorate in American church history. Author of* Anointed to Serve *(1971), the commissioned history of the Assemblies of God, Menzies cofounded (with Vinson Synan and Horace Ward in 1970) the Society of Pentecostal Studies, and was its first president and the first editor of its journal,* Pneuma. *A participant in the Lausanne Consultation (1984), he is a respected interpreter of Pentecostal theology.*

J. I. Packer *is professor of historical and systematic theology at Regent College, Vancouver, British Columbia. He is a graduate of Oxford University, from which he received a D.Phil. His many books include* "Fundamentalism" and the Word of God *(Eerdmans, 1958),* Evangelism and the Sovereignty of God *(InterVarsity, 1961),* Knowing God *(InterVarsity, 1973), and* Keeping in Step with the Spirit *(Revell, 1984).*

Quentin J. Schultze *is professor of communication arts and sciences at Calvin College, Grand Rapids, Michigan. He received his Ph.D. in communications from the University of Illinois in Urbana-Champaign. A frequent contributor to* Christianity Today *magazine, Schultze is the author of* Television: Manna from Hollywood? *(Zondervan, 1987).*

Harold B. Smith *is vice-president/editorial for Christianity Today, Inc. A graduate of the University of Michigan, Smith further studied and taught journalism at Michigan State University. He is a former managing editor of* Christianity Today *magazine; and for six years served the National Association of Evangelicals as director of information.*

Russell P. Spittler *is professor of New Testament and director of the David du Plessis Center for Christian Spirituality at Fuller Theological Seminary, Pasadena, California. A graduate of Southeastern Bible Institute (now Southeastern College), Florida Southern College, Wheaton College, and Gordon-Conwell Theological Seminary, Spittler received his doctorate from Harvard University. He is a frequent contributor to magazines and theological journals and has published a number of* *books, including* Cults and Isma *(Baker Book House, ninth printing, 1977) and* Perspectives on the New Pentecostalism *Baker Book House, 1976).*

Vinson Synan *is chairman of the North American Renewal Service Committee. He is a graduate of the University of Richmond and the University of Georgia, from which he earned a master's degree in history and a doctorate in U.S. social and intellectual history. A former pastor, Synan is the author of numerous books, including* The Holiness-Pentecostal Movement in the U.S. *(Eerdmans, 1971) and* The Twentieth-Century Pentecostal Explosion *(Creation House, 1987).*